VILLA
IN THE BLOOD

VILLA
IN THE BLOOD
Bernard Bale

First published in Great Britain in 1998 by
The Breedon Books Publishing Company Limited

This paperback edition published in Great Britain in 2015 by DB
Publishing, an imprint of JMD Media Ltd

ISBN 978-1-78091-471-8

Printed and bound in the UK by Copytech (UK) Ltd Peterborough

CONTENTS

ACKNOWLEDGEMENT

The Author wishes to thank Neil Rioch for
his great help with information and
interviews, and, of course, everyone else who
contributed both their time and efforts in the
common cause of rejoicing in the Aston Villa
Football Club.

INTRODUCTION

IF ONLY Villa Park could talk, what stories it could tell. For more than a century this wonderful stadium has witnessed the most amazing football days and nights, cheers, tears, fears, triumphs, failures and frustrations. It has been graced by legends and soccer talent that would surely hang in the National Gallery were their art expressed on canvas rather than on grass.

Sadly, Villa Park cannot talk. It is simply the skeleton, the fine frame upon which proudly stands one of the most famous bodies in world football — the unique Aston Villa. No, the skeleton cannot talk but the flesh and blood of that body certainly can. Villa people are the flesh and blood of the club, as indeed, the club has become part of their own flesh and blood in a bonding of passion that lasts a lifetime. Once a Villa man or woman, always a Villa man or woman.

Aston Villa goes back to an October evening in 1874. The month matters little but the evening matters a great deal because on that evening four members of the Villa Cross Wesleyan Chapel Cricket Club were having a chat under a street gas-light about the unofficial game of football that they had been watching a few hours earlier. They were enthusiastic about what they had seen because, while cricket remained their first love, they wanted something to do in the winter which would keep them all together.

"Why don't we start our own football team?" Suggested one.

"There are enough of us in the cricket club and we can always find a few more if some of the others aren't keen," agreed another.

It was at that moment that euphoria took over from enthusiasm and Aston Villa was born into a Victorian world in which Red Indians were still fighting the encroaching palefaces, Brahms was still alive and the FA Cup was not yet two years old.

Villa's first game was unusual to say the least as they took on St Mary's Aston Brook — one of the area's leading RUGBY teams! The first half of the game was played under rugby rules with an oval ball and the second half under the existing soccer rules with a round one. The ball was hired for the occasion for the sum of one shilling and sixpence, which was quite expensive then although it is only seven pence in today's money. There was no score by half-time but in the second half the newly-formed Aston Villa side pulled off a 1-0 win. Considering that the teams were 15-a-side and that there were seven forwards in each team, it is quite a surprise that there was only one goal.

The following season organisation set in. The club had become official on that very first night under the street lamp when those present each put a shilling in the kitty to help set everything up. Now, fixtures had to be arranged and there were a series of friendlies played at Aston Park in the shadow of the stately Aston Hall, which had been under attack by the Roundheads during Cromwellian days and was now under siege from the round ball!

The name George Ramsey became synonymous with Aston

Villa in later years as the club prospered, but his initial involvement with the club came as something of an accident. He stopped to watch a game in Aston Park and realised that Villa were a man short. He was a Scot who had learned his football in Glasgow and he could not resist asking if he could play. Not only did he play but his performance was so outstanding that he was made captain there and then, thus beginning a career with the club which eventually took him through 46 years, not only as an excellent player but also as an energetic administrator.

When Villa rented a butcher's field in which to play their games, they began to charge admission. Spectators paid three pence for the privilege and the first game yielded five shillings and three pence — which meant that the official attendance figure was just 21. That was in 1876 but it was not long before the club began to hit the big time.

In 1880 they won the Birmingham Senior Cup to capture their very first serious honour. They also entered the FA Cup for the first time, which was another step up the ladder. In 1885 professionalism in football was legalised and as the game began to take off, so Villa took off with it. In 1887 they won the FA Cup with a thrilling 2-0 win over Midlands rivals West Bromwich Albion at the Oval, and a year later they were among the founder-members of the Football League which had been pioneered by a Birmingham draper by the name of William McGregor — who was also a very active member of the Aston Villa committee.

The rise of Aston Villa was breathtaking. In the remaining years of the 19th century they were winners of the FA Cup twice more and were League champions on no fewer than five occasions. Their 1896-97 season was particularly outstanding because they became only the second club to achieve the magnificent double of League and FA Cup success — a feat that was not to be emulated for another 64 years.

There were other events which grabbed newspaper headlines for the club. The double triumph was celebrated for months in the Midlands and then the FA Cup was put on display in a shop window — and was stolen! Happier headlines came in April 1897 when they played their first game in their wonderful new stadium, Villa Park.

The century changed but Villa continued on the same path of success, winning the FA Cup again in 1905, 1913 and 1920. They were also League champions again in 1910 and, during the remaining years leading up to World War Two, they supplied many internationals to the home countries. There was a blip when they slipped into the Second Division, but they soon bounced back and were still considered among the biggest clubs in Europe when the whistle was blown on football and war abruptly interrupted the lives of the entire nation.

The war badly affected the population but could not extinguish the spirit. Aston Villa blew the rubble dust from its silverware cabinet and vowed to again win those trophies that mean so much. That vow was fulfilled, the mission accomplished both here in Britain and overseas as Villa went beyond their wildest dreams and became Kings of Europe.

Villa Park cannot tell the story but its flesh and blood can as we pick up the story of Aston Villa in the days since World War Two. The wonders and the woes are relived by those who know — because they were there and, in many cases, are still there! And they all have Villa in the Blood.

CHAPTER ONE

AN OUTBREAK OF PEACE

THE bells were ringing and there was dancing in the battered streets of Birmingham when World War Two finally ended and peace was restored. For years there had been the pounding of bombs and guns, marching feet, the crashing of falling buildings and the awful pain of bereavement. The city of Birmingham had gritted its teeth along with the rest of the country, determined to smile through the pain barrier even though its eyes were moist.

There had, of course, been wartime football among the many other distractions aimed at keeping morale high and life as near normal as possible. Yet it was a mere skeleton of the real thing and had simply provided a temporary diversion rather than a real distraction. When darkness fell and the drone of the approaching bombers was heralded by the wailing of the sirens, there was little more thought than the desire to survive the night and see the sunrise of the next day. That is why the world opened its eyes to the dawn of peace and took a wonderful gulp of fresh air. It was good to be alive.

They turned up in their tens of thousands at Villa Park to celebrate the rebirth of serious soccer. For several seasons there had been a League North and a League South and the people of the Midlands could have been excused for thinking, "What about us?" This was all the more reasonable because then, as now, there were certainly enough contenders in the centre of the land to have warranted a league of their own. However, this no longer mattered. It was now August 1946 and football was back! The gardens around Villa Park were blooming and attendances inside the ground were blooming also.

In the last season before football re-opened for serious business Villa were runners-up in the League South — a cause for greater celebration had it not been for the fact that rivals, Birmingham, were the champions of that 1945-46 season. That particular season was also famous for a massive crowd on Saturday, 2 March when Derby County visited for the first of a two-leg FA Cup sixth-round tie. Villa Park was bursting at the seams as 76,588 fans squeezed themselves into the ground. Interestingly, the receipts for that huge crowd were just £8,651 2s 6d — which would probably not even meet the average salary of a Villa player of today.

There are still those around who were there when all this was going on, among them Harry Parkes. Harry was Erdington-born and a Villa man since he joined them as an amateur in 1939 from Boldmere St Michael's. Essentially a right-half he played in every position for Villa including emergency goalkeeper. But for injury he would surely have won England caps. As it was he became legendary at Villa Park and not only for his playing skills.

"I suppose I was what they used to call a bit of a character. I didn't like to take life too seriously and I liked to have a bit of fun. It was always good for team spirit. After those war years it was good to be able to laugh.

"On the train I used to wait until everyone was dozing — other passengers as well as the Villa lads — then I would shout, "All tickets please!" It was great to watch them all fumbling through their pockets for their tickets. I remember planting a load of cutlery in a reporter's bag once and then tipping off the railway police that he had taken it all from the dining car.

"I used to get it back, though. I put on a disguise when we were playing away to Manchester City. I got a false nose, false moustache and a homburg hat, just to wind up the commissionaire. When I took them off he wouldn't believe that I was a Villa player and it took the manager and a couple of the directors to talk him into letting me in.

"The other lads got their own back as well. We were on a train coming back from a friendly against Hearts in Edinburgh. I fell asleep and when the lads woke me up and told me we were at Crewe, I had no reason to doubt it. I got off the train to get some tea from the kiosk when, to my horror, the train moved off with the lads waving cheerio to me. There I was, in my shirtsleeves with just a few coppers in my pocket, marooned on a railway platform in Preston! It was three o'clock in the morning before I finally made it back to Birmingham."

Harry Parkes also remembers what it was like to be back in business in August 1946 when the temporary competitions ended and once again the Football League and the FA Cup were back in full swing (although the Cup had begun again the previous year).

"My greatest memory of the post-war period was the size of the crowds. They were huge. It was amazing to stand on the pitch and look around at so many people — and only two policemen too! We didn't look upon ourselves as stars in those days. When I was playing I used to travel to Villa Park on the bus the same as everyone else. Can you imagine today's Villa players doing that? They would never be able to get off the bus because of all the autograph hunters.

"I would love to be playing today. It is a great game. I owe everything I have to football and I wish I could have gone on playing for ever. I often wonder what it would be like to play in today's boots, and kick or head today's footballs. They are so very different — and probably much better.

"I still watch Villa when I can get to the ground but, to be honest, I am a bit of an addict to televised football. I watch game after game and drive my wife mad. I believe that the players of my era would do just as well today. I can't see the likes of Matthews, Finney, Lawton and my own Villa mates not being successful in the game today. Talent is talent no matter in what era you are playing.

"I was a toolmaker, now I am a retired footballer with a sports outfitters that has served me well since I gave up playing. I stayed at Villa to play a part behind the scenes because I wanted to give something back to the club that has always meant so much to me. Let's face it …I'm just a big fan really!"

In the Villa goal just after the war was Alan Wakeman who had been at the club since joining them in 1935 at the age of 15. He was a schoolboy international and had gradually been elevated from the Villa 'A' team to the Reserves and then finally, in 1938, to the first team where he played in six senior matches before the war intervened.

During the war he guested for other teams, including Nottingham Forest and Notts County, but, like the rest of the world, he could not wait for peace to return.

"Those were dark days. We still had our football, but it was nothing like it had been before the war. Sport and entertainment kept up people's spirits but you never knew from one game to the next if you were ever going to see the same player again. Football became the nation's escape and, whether you were just watching or playing, it was something that we all looked forward to.

"We all went a little bit crazy when peace finally arrived. The dark days were over and the lights came on again. I resumed playing for Villa and the atmosphere at Villa Park was just fantastic. Those were very exciting days. The crowds were huge and when you went out on to the pitch all you could see on all four sides was a mass of faces. There were tens of thousands of people there and it could be quite daunting if you let it get to you.

"There was a great atmosphere in the dressing-room. We were all happy to be there with things getting back to normal — and I think we were all a little relieved as well, relieved that we had survived.

"It was all very different then. The game was different, the supporters were different, we were different. One of my old aunts used to give me old jerseys and shorts for training in. Can you imagine that being necessary now?

"Transport was different too. We went by train or bus to some of our games — but sometimes we went by car. I can remember when we played away to Wolves one Christmas and there was no transport available — public or otherwise. Jack Morby and I went on a tandem together. We got there in time, played the game and then cycled all the way home again. Physiotherapists would have a fit if their players did anything like that today.

"Most of us had other jobs too — many working down the pits. You had to! It wasn't possible to survive on a footballer's wage in those days. We used to train a couple of days a week while holding down our jobs. When Saturday came, though, we suddenly became stars. People who worked alongside us during the week would cheer us on at the weekend as if we had never met. Some of them even asked us for our autographs."

Aston Villa had a big reputation during those post-war years. Their successes throughout the previous decades had made them one of the teams that everyone else wanted to conquer. Their profile had even been perpetuated during the war when they won the Football League (North) War Cup in May 1944. Perhaps that doesn't sound such a big deal? If you think that, then Alan Wakeman might change your mind.

"We met Blackpool in the Final and they were a very strong side in those days. They were certainly strong enough to beat us in the first leg at Bloomfield Road. We came home on the wrong end of a 2-1 scoreline and we knew they were not going to be pushovers the following week when we were to play the second leg at Villa Park."

The second leg turned out to be one of the most exciting games ever witnessed at Villa Park. Ask any of the 55,000 who were there.

"There was a lot of pride at stake. We just couldn't allow Blackpool to be presented with the Cup on our own ground and so we went into the game with our sleeves rolled up. Blackpool were the League champions but we were determined that they would not take the Cup as well. We tore into them from the start but they gave as good as they got and within a quarter of an hour we had scored two each.

"Just before half-time Bob Iverson made it 3-2 to us so,

when we went back to the dressing-room, we were level on aggregate. We had only been playing for a few minutes into the second half when Frank Broome scored and we were 5-4 ahead on aggregate. Blackpool threw everything at us after that but we held firm and we won the Cup. It was a great game and a great experience. We were not given medals but we did receive tankards. I still have mine!"

Alan Wakeman's career did not extend much beyond the immediate post-war years. He was among those who had been cheated of greater glory by the advent of that greater conflict. However he carries no feelings of bitterness.

"My only regret is that I could not play for longer. I ate too many doughnuts — they were a weakness of mine — and I think they helped me to get too big and too fat. Had I been more careful I might have lasted a year or two longer. Still, I certainly have nothing but happy memories of my time at Aston Villa.

"I played more than 200 matches in the peace years. In fact I only missed three because of a broken jaw in one long spell. I travelled and had some great experiences with Villa and enjoyed every single minute of it. We were all good pals and I shared many happy times with blokes like Jack Morby, Eddie and Reg Lowe, Jackie Maund, Amos Moss, George Cummings, Billy Goffin and all the others. We were all mates together and we all shared the same desire to enjoy ourselves, enjoy our football and, most of all, to enjoy being Aston Villa players. Of course I would love to be playing for Villa today, but I would not have missed those days at Villa Park for anything."

Those words are echoed by 'Sailor' Brown, a tricky winger who spent most of his post-war career at Villa Park although he also suffered as a result of the war. Robert Brown had been a Villa fan for years before he joined the club.

"Billy Walker was my idol when I was a kid. I thought he was brilliant and I still do. I was a very keen Villa fan even though I was born and brought up in Gorleston. I used to go to school with George Edwards who was later a team-mate when we were both at Villa Park.

"After I finished at Villa I returned to Gorleston and became player-manager of our local side, but those were happy days for me at Aston Villa. The club treated me very well and I still keep in touch even though I don't see them play as often as I would like."

Robert Brown, sometimes called Albert, had the nickname 'Sailor' bestowed upon him because he had, what he himself describes as, a 'nautical' gait. He was involved in some of the post-war classic games of Villa. He had previously been with Charlton Athletic and had also played during the war years for both England and the RAF.

"Leslie Smith was a pal and a team-mate in the wartime England and RAF games and we both later joined Villa. Leslie had been a left-winger with Brentford and when I arrived at Villa Park we soon picked up where we had left off during the war. He had the No 11 shirt and I had the No 10. I was used to big crowds because of my days at Charlton so it was nothing new for me to be playing in front of fifty or sixty thousand. However, playing for Villa was very special. This was my dream team. Possibly my best years were already behind me but joining up with Villa was almost like starting my career all over again. I was like a big kid when I sat in the Villa dressing-room for the first time — it meant so much to me.

"We certainly had some epic games, especially Cup games and local derbies. I think that the passion for football in the Midlands has often been overlooked because of what you hear about Merseyside or Manchester but, when I was playing for Aston Villa, you could feel the will of the supporters and I'm sure it feels the same for the players at Villa Park today.

"The game was different in those days. People say that it is faster today but I'm not so sure. If it is, then you have to take into consideration that we probably played on heavier pitches then, the boots were more for hard work than for sprinting and the ball itself was much heavier — especially when it was muddy. It was like heading a cannonball sometimes and I have noticed that a number of the players whose particular talent or job involved a lot of heading have since died of Alzheimer's disease. I don't know if there is really any connection — but if not then it is quite a coincidence.

"If I have a criticism of today's game it is that there are too many show-offs and continentals. It is not the same. Having said that, there are some great players around at the moment. I don't know if they are any better than the Lawtons, Carters or Matthews, but they are just as entertaining. I would not want to be playing today myself. No thank you! I enjoyed my years in the game — especially those at Aston Villa where I was at my happiest — but I would not want to be playing today. There are far too many pressures.

"There were pressures when I was playing but they were all confined to the game itself. I would not have minded a fiver for every time a big defender would whisper in my ear early in the game: "You're not here for long." That was part of the game then and I know that it still is. You had your good games and your bad games but there were not the huge amounts of money at stake as there are today and therefore whatever pressure you were under was just for the 90 minutes that you were playing."

Sailor Brown is still living in Gorleston and is now aged 82.

He avidly follows Villa through television but only occasionally makes the trip to Villa Park.

"I would be there every week if I could. It is all a far cry from my days of being paid £15 a week to pull on the Aston Villa shirt, but I have nothing but the happiest of memories of those special times. I was born to play for Aston Villa. They were really the only club for me and they still are. To be there during those wonderful days after World War Two when everyone had a smile on their face was a great experience. I can still see and hear everyone laughing and joking in the dressing-room. Many of them have passed away now but they are still very much alive in my memory. A great bunch of fellows — but then, they would be — they were playing for Aston Villa."

During those boom years of the 1940s Villa were trying hard to reassemble. Alex Massie had become manager in 1945 and, as he tried to revamp the side to recapture the glory he had experienced as a player and captain, there were some heart-stopping moments.

"We seemed to get into the habit of having a bad start to the season and looking certainties for relegation, only to play like champions in the second half of the season and finish in a respectable position," said Alan Wakeman.

It was a habit that certainly drove everyone to distraction and yet the Villa board did not seem to mind too much and Alex Massie remained as manager until 1950. During that time, Villa finished eighth in the 1946-47 season, sixth in the 1947-48 season, tenth in the 1948-49 season and twelfth in the 1949-50 season.

What a difference the top division was in those days with Portsmouth twice winning the championship, Manchester United finishing as runners-up for three out of four seasons, and clubs like Brentford, Grimsby, Fulham and Blackpool all featuring in the First Division.

Perhaps Villa's problem was that while the side was long in experience, there was a shortfall of youth and the legs grew tired too quickly. Certainly, in terms of results, they had seen better days — and there were to be greater days for the club in the decades that lay ahead. However, in those days of Woodbines, ration books and bags of roasted peanuts, results played second fiddle to the sheer joy of being there, at Villa Park.

The faces have changed since those wonder years of the post-war period but the spirit remains the same. After the storm of war the world was smiling again in the face of a new dawn and the dew of peace. At Villa Park that new dawn manifested itself in huge crowds, epic matches, great characters and, for some, the happiest days of their lives.

CHAPTER TWO

VILLA PARK

THERE is no doubt that Villa Park is one of the finest stadiums in the land — but that is hardly news. It always has been rather special. In fact, it is a reflection of the positive attitude that the world of football has come to expect from Aston Villa.

It was back in 1896 when the need for a better ground first arose — but there was the obvious snag — money! The committee running the club realised that something quite spectacular had to be arranged if Villa were to keep making progress and afford a new ground. It was at that moment that someone proposed making Aston Villa a private limited company. A subsequent share issue raised £10,000 and, on the back of that, a lease was arranged for the use of Aston Lower Grounds, a former amusement park.

Aston Lower Grounds was quite amazing. Not even Wembley or Old Trafford nearing the 21st century can boast the facilities of Villa's new home in the latter part of the 19th. It had an ornamental lake, aquarium, skating rink, concert hall, rifle range, tea rooms, bowling greens, tennis courts and landscaped gardens. It was the Alton Towers of its day!

Through the years, of course, Villa Park has undergone many changes. In those early days a football pitch had to be created — and where better than on one of the lakes! As various parts of the Aston Lower Grounds vanished, so a new sports ground was gradually created. Around the pitch a concrete cycle track was laid — although it had a relatively short life since, in 1913, it was removed to allow for greater spectator capacity.

The new Aston Lower Grounds Football Stadium hosted its first official game on 17 August 1897. Blackburn Rovers were the visitors and Villa, fittingly, won 3-0. A century later, on 13 August 1997 to be precise, Blackburn were again the visitors — this time for a Premiership match. Villa lost 4-0 — no way to celebrate a centenary!

The demand to see Villa just grew and grew and with that demand came the necessity for further changes at the stadium. In 1923, as economic depression loomed throughout Europe, the club found itself in a position to spend £25,000 on a new stand at the Trinity Road end. Not only did it improve spectator facilities but it also created new treatment and dressing-rooms.

While the city of Birmingham was really hammered by German bombs during the war, Villa Park emerged unscathed — despite the Trinity Road stand being used as an air-raid shelter and the home dressing-room being occupied by a rifle company of the 9th Battalion of the Royal Warwickshire Regiment. Every few years further work has been done enabling the stadium to continue as one of the leading grounds in Britain. It is hardly recognisable now as the one-time amusement and leisure park. One of the last vestiges to go was the bowling green — but finally, in 1966, even that had to make way for a new social club. The main entrance to Villa Park is itself a tribute to days gone by. What now constitutes offices was once the aquarium. Like football itself the stadium has geared up for the next century. On the crest of a boom Villa Park has been transformed regularly to keep up with the rigours and demands of today's football. The regular investments have paid off as the ground was used in both the 1966 World Cup and Euro '96, and the international coaches and managers who have flocked there have all been very complimentary about the ground and its playing surface.

"We were delighted to be at Villa Park for Euro '96 group games," said Scotland manager Craig Brown. "It is an excellent stadium, steeped in history, yet as modern as you could possibly want. We were very happy with the condition of the pitch and we won one and drew one of our two games so we were unbeaten there. The Tartan Army loved the place too and we would certainly be happy to play there again if a similar occasion arose. Villa Park is a great ground and a credit to a great club."

As well as two Group A matches, Villa Park hosted the quarter-final game between Czechoslovakia and Portugal. Karel Poborsky, later to join Manchester United, was the Czech hero of the day when he scored the only goal of the game with a magnificent chip over the head of Portuguese 'keeper, Baia, after a solo break from midfield.

"It was a great occasion for me and I was all the more confident because we were playing at Villa Park. The conditions were exactly as I like them and there was a lot of support for us. The dressing-rooms and facilities were first class and we all felt very good before the game. It was a great experience," said Poborsky.

His words echoed those of the stars who had played at Villa Park in 1966 when the ground hosted the World Cup Group 2 matches between Argentina and Spain, West Germany and Argentina, and West Germany and Spain.

"It was a good choice for us," said Franz Beckenbauer. "We played two of our group games there and one at Sheffield. Our biggest win was at Sheffield, but we played our best football at Aston Villa. I remember that it was a nice stadium and that the support was very good there. Villa Park was a very good English ground with the kind of surface that was much better for us than for Argentina or Spain. I really wish that the Final had been held there as I think we might have won."

Yes, Villa Park has played host to some illustrious company. The ground's participation in Euro '96 was a huge success with 98,576 people attending the three games. There is little doubt that the stadium will be one of the first on the list for any potential World Cup tournament to be held in England in the future. The ground has an excellent reputation with the Football Association, which is why it is a regular venue for FA Cup semi-finals and has hosted no less than nine England internationals down the decades.

"There is no doubt that Villa Park is one of the best grounds in the country," said FA chief executive Graham Kelly. "It is ideally placed for travelling supporters and is run very professionally. That is why it is in regular use by the Football Association. We like to stage matches at stadiums which are professionally run, have a good capacity and the facilities and experience to cope with big occasions. Villa Park fits very comfortably into that category."

When the club staged their first match at Villa Park, 15,000 turned up to watch. Today's attendances average 36,000. Shaun Teale played 175 senior games for Aston Villa during the first half of the 1990s and loved the place.

"People used to say that the best stadiums were at Liverpool and Manchester United, but Villa invested heavily in their ground as they have done continually down the years and, apart from the actual capacity, I don't think that Villa Park can be excluded from the list of Britain's top ten grounds.

"The changing rooms are particularly good with lots of space. They were refurbished during my time and what had been the visitors' dressing-room was enlarged and changed to the home dressing-room. The atmosphere at Villa Park is always great. There's nothing to touch an evening match under floodlights with a capacity crowd. I'd buy a ticket for that myself!"

Stan Collymore considers Villa Park to be his second home.

"When I signed for Villa from Liverpool it really was like coming home. I know that sounds like an old cliché but remember, I used to come here when I was a kid. I always supported Villa and I was just like all the other star-struck kids twenty years ago, getting here early to get a good place and then watching the ground fill up before the players came out.

"Villa Park has changed a bit since then. There used to be standing in those days. The ground was always better than most but now it is a real super stadium. I have some great memories of players and games here but mostly I think that Villa Park was just the place where you wanted to be. There was a sense of belonging. I think that's why, when I came here after joining from Liverpool, I was quite nervous. Playing here as an opponent was completely different because it was just another game and you were totally focussed on getting the points but, having it as my home ground and knowing that I was playing in front of a lot of the people I grew up with, was a completely different prospect.

"I was once asked if I thought that Villa Park could become the Old Trafford of the Midlands. It was a difficult one for me to answer because, to me, it always has been. Midlands football has often been overlooked. When people come to Villa Park for the first time they often seem surprised at how good the ground is. I don't know what they expected because Villa Park has been one of the top grounds in the country for generations.

"There has always been a great atmosphere here, even during the days when things were not going so well. It would have taken something very exciting for me to leave Liverpool but, when I first heard that I might be on my way to Villa, I couldn't believe it. I would not have been happier if someone had told me that I might have won the lottery. Playing here is a dream come true and I hope it will go on for the rest of my career. I love the stadium, I love the area, and I love the people. This is home to me."

Tony Daley was at Villa Park for ten years as a player but before that he was also one of the lads who stood regularly at the Holte End.

"I was a bit of a late starter in some ways because, although I was born and brought up just a few minutes from the ground, I used to follow whichever club was at the top of the League. Then, when I was eleven, I went with my brother to see Villa play and I was hooked. I loved going to Villa Park it was such a terrific ground. I even went to reserve games!

"The atmosphere at the ground was always great, it's that kind of a stadium. I remember going to see Villa play Ipswich in a crunch game that looked as if it might settle the championship. We were top and Ipswich were a close second. The place was absolutely packed. I got there early but so did everyone else and, although I did get into the ground and stood at the Holte End, I did not see one second of the game. I was too small and could only hear what was going on. I didn't mind a bit because it was just so good to be there. There were nearly 47,500 in the ground, Gary Shaw scored for us but Ipswich hit two and took the points. It looked as if we might have blown our title chance but in the remaining few matches the results went Villa's way and I remember watching the League championship trophy paraded around the ground. I was fourteen at the time.

"That season the attendances at Villa Park were third only to Manchester United and Liverpool — and that's how I see Villa's status in the game, the third biggest club. When I became a player it was the highlight of my life. I have stood on the pitch and looked at the place where I used to stand and reminded myself of how lucky I am. There are thousands of kids who dream of playing professionally, many of them for Villa. I was one of the lucky ones.

"The stadium did not change a great deal during my time but there has been a lot of investment since. I still go to Villa Park whenever there is a chance and I still cheer them on. I began as a fan and I am still a fan. For me Villa Park is so special that I enjoy being there even when there is no game on."

If there is one man who knows the ground better than most then that man must be Ted Small, stadium manager at Villa Park, who has been involved with the club for more than thirty years.

"I came here by accident really. I was born and bred in Walsall and of course that was my team. However, I am a builder by trade and it was my work that brought me here — although not in the way you might expect. I was working on a garage when I got talking to Joe Rutherford, the former Villa player. Joe played for the team just before the war and then again for about six years after it.

"We were chatting away about football and he was still connected with Villa and offered me a couple of complimentary tickets for a game. I took him up on his kind offer and took my son along. He was seven or eight at the time. It was the start of a season and the weather was lovely. The pitch looked beautiful with the stark white lines standing out against the lush green of the grass. It just looked the perfect place to be on that Saturday afternoon and I was hooked. I fell in love with Villa Park there and then and started to follow the team — even though I have always enjoyed a game of football for its own sake rather than to get into all the facts and figures and blinkered approach that some people seem to enjoy. The sheer joy of football is what appeals to me.

"If I remember correctly Tommy Docherty hadn't been manager for very long so this was in 1968. I began to attend Villa matches regularly and, when I heard that some changes were being planned for the ground, I offered my services to Mr Ellis. I wasn't looking for any payment, I just wanted to help.

"I started to come into the ground early before a game and check all the plumbing and heating and generally make myself available for any handyman jobs that needed doing. Over the years I got more and more involved. Then there was some unrest at the club around 1980 and I stopped being involved behind the scenes. I still followed the Villa though.

"Then Mr Ellis returned as chairman and I rejoined on a full-time basis. Now, I am stadium manager and responsible for all aspects regarding the upkeep of the ground. It was me who built the Trinity Road stand. We run our own building firm within the club and, by doing that instead of going to outside contractors, we saved about £2 million. There are lots of jobs to do all the time and we must have saved an incredible amount of money over the years by having our own building operation.

"I can remember when the fencing around the ground came down after the Taylor Report that we found ourselves in the ridiculous situation of having to put fencing up one week, knowing that we would have to pull it all down again the following week. The laws were about to be passed but had not yet become legal and, for our safety certificates, we had to comply with the existing laws. It was not a problem that was exclusive to Villa. Most clubs had the same problem but there was no alternative — and that wasted a lot of time, effort and money.

"I was opposed to all-seater stadiums when the idea was first mooted. I thought that a lot of the atmosphere would be gone if you did away with the standing areas — but I've since changed my mind about that. In the old days, once you were on the terraces and in place you couldn't move. If you wanted a cup of tea or to go to the toilet you were stuck and had to do without. Today, with comfortable seating, easy access and much better facilities, life is much better for spectators and I'm sure that the atmosphere has not declined at all. There is still talk of returning to standing on the terraces, but I don't think that the new stands could take it. They are built for people to sit down and if they were asked to accommodate a greater number of people who are standing up and jumping about I don't think the footings would be able to take it.

"As well as Villa games we have had some other memorable occasions here at Villa Park. I have been here for pop concerts with people like Barry White, Duran Duran and others and thoroughly enjoyed them. We have had boxing here and religious gatherings which are always interesting.

"I have seen great players like Pele and Beckenbauer on our pitch and I have shared a joke with many famous footballers and managers — including our own Villa managers. I don't think I have ever had anything less than a good relationship with any of the Villa managers. Mind you, they always want more from me than I do from them, so perhaps that has something to do with it!

"If I had to pick a highlight I think it would probably be the Scotland versus Holland game in Euro '96. That was a great game to watch and both sides performed really well. There was a fantastic atmosphere among the supporters as well as the two teams and their officials, and it was a real pleasure to have the game played here. It was a tremendous advertisement for football and, if anyone was going to see a game for the first time, especially with their family, I am sure they would have been very impressed with the whole thing.

"One of the best Villa games was a Cup-tie against Tranmere a few years ago. It was a real heart-in-the-mouth game. One minute we were ahead and the next we were behind and the last twenty minutes were just amazing. In the end it went to penalties and we got through but there were a lot of very weary people trooping out of Villa Park — and that was just the spectators who were totally exhausted from watching!"

Someone once described the running of a successful football club as being like a swan on the water. It appears to be gliding along nicely with very little apparent effort, but beneath the surface of the water there is a lot of frantic paddling going on. A football club is definitely like that. When you turn up to see a game there are always enough players, clean shirts and shorts, and an abundance of meat pies and cups of tea. Yet none of this has happened by pure chance.

Let's take the kit as an example. Jim Paul has been responsible for the Villa players being well turned-out for some years — and it is a job that he loves.

"Playing for Villa means that you are a top professional and so everything about you must be absolutely right," says Jim. "I use as much kit and accessories for a home game as I do for an away match. The gear is all kept at our Bodymoor training ground, so on a match-day I turn up with just as many hangers as the opposition!"

Jim has a check-list for every game and, even though he knows it all by heart, he still goes meticulously through the kit for every single match.

"I leave nothing to chance, especially for away games. I have a word with the opposition and the referee before every away match just to make sure that we avoid any shirt clashes. It's not just taking care of the kit for the team as a whole, but also meeting the special needs of individual players. Some players prefer long sleeves, while others prefer short. When Dean Saunders was here he used to play the first half in short sleeves and then change at half-time. You have to know about these things. It isn't just for the first team either, the kit responsibility is also for the Reserves and the various youth teams."

Jim also found himself with an added responsibility a few years ago when he and his family played host to Jamie Major, son of the then Prime Minister, who was having a trial with Villa.

"Jamie is football-crazy and this was the first professional club that he came to. We knew who his father was, of course, but we didn't treat him any differently to the other trialists who stay with us. He didn't ask for any favours and we didn't give him any. He was a nice lad and he wrote to us a little later on to say thank you.

"The biggest thrill associated with that episode came when we were playing away to Arsenal. After the game I was invited to the VIP Guests' Lounge. I wondered what was going on and was finally told, 'The Prime Minister would like to meet you.' I went up and had a ten-minute chat with him. He walked right over to me when I came into the Lounge and would not allow anyone to distract him. He was a very pleasant chap and put me at my ease almost immediately. We talked about football of course but, since he had only been Prime Minister for about six months at that time, I asked him how he was getting on and we chatted about that for a while too. We had a few laughs and I think one or two in the room were beginning to wonder who on earth I was.

"When I arrived home at about two in the morning, my wife Sylvia was still awake. She was amazed when I told her what had happened and I think we spent the rest of the night talking about it. It was a great experience."

There's not much point in keeping a racehorse if you are not going to keep him in tip-top condition. Exactly the same applies to footballers. There would be no point in spending millions on top players only to neglect their health. That is why Villa Park's physiotherapist is such an important member of the behind-the-scenes staff. Villa's Jim Walker remains one of the best-known and most popular in British football. A former player himself, he always took a keen interest in physio work.

"I stopped playing in 1981. I might have gone on a little longer but I had an Achilles problem and decided that, at the age of 33, there was little point in hanging on. I decided that the time would be put to better use if I embarked on my physio ambitions. I had already done the FA course and I found a job straight away in Kuwait with Dave Mackay. I had an interesting two years there followed by a couple of years at Blackburn before Graham Taylor invited me to join Villa.

"This is a tremendous club and I am very happy here. The facilities and atmosphere in the dressing-rooms are excellent. I am very pleased that I chose to be a physio rather than going into management. When I am on the bench I am very relaxed. I am busy watching the players for any signs of knocks or strains so I never get uptight about the results or any referee's decisions. Don't get me wrong. I always want Villa to do well, but my job is to care for the players and that is what is important.

"The most rewarding part is when I see a player return to form after a bad injury. Sometimes a player may look like he will never walk again let alone play football. He puts his confidence in you and you get him back to full health — not just by physical treatment but by encouragement through talking, coaxing, letting him know that you have been through it all yourself. Players get very low when they have been injured as you might imagine, but you can build up a unique relationship with them and sometimes give them back their careers.

"I've got a bit of a reputation at Villa for a dry sense of humour, but nothing makes me grin more than when a player who has been through a major injury scores a brilliant goal or makes a fantastic save. I believe I have the best job in the game and I hope that the Villa Park treatment room will be my domain for as long as possible."

Another familiar face from behind the scenes is that of Abdul Rashid, Aston Villa's commercial manager. One of Abdul's predecessors was Tony Stephens, one of the game's leading consultants and also advisor to stars like Alan Shearer, David Platt, Dwight Yorke, David Beckham and Michael Owen. It was Tony Stephens who gave Abdul a grounding in the job.

The role of the commercial manager has changed dramatically in the last 50 years. During the post-war boom time, few clubs had a commercial manager. Someone would arrange fund-raising prize draw tickets but that was about it. The club secretary often took on responsibility for advertising boards around the ground and space in the programme. However, as the financial aspect of the game mushroomed into today's highly-charged commercialism, clubs came to realise that someone needed to be taking complete responsibility for that side of potential income. That "someone" is now a complete department at most clubs. Aston Villa are no exception.

"Working for Villa is just fantastic for me," said Abdul. "I have been a fan all my life. I used to stand at the Holte End when I was a schoolboy and I hardly ever missed a game, whether it was the first team or the Reserves. I just loved to be at Villa Park — it was my second home. I never expected to be a professional footballer — I knew that was never going to happen — but I was a ball-boy here and used to help out fetching and carrying wherever I could. I even used to clean the cars of some of the players. It was my way of being a part of the team at my favourite club!

"I was at a loose end when I left school. I had hoped for a career as a draughtsman until I discovered that there was a lot more to that than I had anticipated. The Villa Shop was looking for a full-time assistant, so I applied. When they interviewed me they asked me about my ambitions. I said that I wanted to be commercial manager. It seemed a distant dream at that time but I was given the job in the shop and that set me on the road towards it.

"I learned a lot from Tony Stephens when he became commercial manager of the club. He left to take up a similar position at Wembley and eventually I took over from Chris Rodman and became commercial manager of Aston Villa. I had fulfilled my ambition — but I was still only starting.

"I have been commercial manager for ten years now and there are always new challenges, new ideas, new contacts. Aston Villa is a very friendly club, run like a big family. The chairman sets a great example and visitors are often impressed by the atmosphere and attitude here. They expect such a big club to be much more formal. For me, Villa Park is still my second home and so I like the commercial department to have a homely feel!

"I hope to be here for ever. I could never imagine myself at another club. I have travelled through relegation and the European Cup with this club and whenever I walk around the stadium I still get the same thrill as when I was standing at the Holte End. I am a Villa fan and I guess I always shall be."

That's a very noticeable aspect of life behind the scenes at Villa Park. Anyone who was not a fan before they joined soon become one — which makes for a great working environment and a brilliant situation in which fans of Aston Villa are catering for other fans of Aston Villa!

And what next for Villa Park?

"There are always changes and improvements being made," said stadium manager, Ted Small. "The stadium is totally different now from its past. There is still a little bit of wall that was once part of the original leisure park but that is all. From the photos I have seen the park was a lovely old place, but then, one day they will probably say the same thing about Villa Park as it is today."

They would be right too — Villa Park is a lovely place!

CHAPTER THREE

DERBY DAYS

THERE is nothing quite like a good derby match to stir the blood, and over the years the rivalry between Aston Villa and Birmingham City has always been with hearts worn on sleeves. Some matches have been tempestuous, others like tidal waves in favour of one side or the other. Never has there been a match which could, by any stretch of the imagination, be called boring.

Birmingham City have been striving for the last few years to get back into the top division and joining battle again with their arch-rivals from Villa Park. Once that happens, both teams will be looking forward to a century of League derby clashes. At the moment the total stands at 96, with Villa having won 39 to Birmingham's 32 — with 25 being drawn.

The word from St Andrew's is that everyone believes that City are as big as Villa and deserve to be alongside them in the Premiership. Villa fans definitely have other ideas and, while they welcome the chance to play against their neighbours, there is no way that they consider themselves to have Birmingham City as their equals. There have, of course, also been some mighty clashes with Wolves, and with West Brom and Coventry, as well as with other sides from the Midlands — but Birmingham City always remains the No 1 enemy.

One of the most thrilling clashes in the history of Villa-City derbies was in the 1925-26 season when the two sides met at Villa Park. Huddersfield were ruling the League in those days but Villa were not too far behind and actually finished in sixth place. Villa had cruised to a 3-0 lead with just over ten minutes left and some fans on both sides, but particularly on the Blues' side, decided that they had had their afternoon's entertainment and were already heading for the trams. What they missed was probably ten of the most exciting football minutes ever witnessed anywhere at any time!

An injury to Dr Victor Milne meant that Villa had to restructure their side for the closing part of the game. Within a minute, the Blues' Joe Bradford latched on to a miskick and pulled back a goal for his side. Two more minutes ticked away and Bradford pounced again, making it 3-2. With six minutes left the Villa goalkeeper, Cyril Spiers, slipped as he stooped to gather a harmless shot and, in his scramble to regain his balance, he inadvertently pushed the ball over the line to make it 3-3. It was an amazing comeback, a fair result in the end, and a game that the spectators talked about well into their years of retirement.

Wolverhampton Wanderers were traditional Christmas opponents for Villa quite often in the past, the two teams sometimes playing each other on both Christmas and Boxing Day. The human fixture organisers were often much kinder than their computer counterparts of today which throw up anti-social engagements on many occasions at times when travel would be better kept to a minimum. For goals the most memorable year was 1933. On the Christmas Day 57,000 fans packed into Villa Park for the visit by Wolves. They were treated to an eight-goal spectacular. Tom 'Pongo' Waring scored twice, Jack Mandley also hit two and Dai Astley and Ronnie Dix scored one each as Villa ran out very convincing 6-2 winners.

The stage was thus set for a great return match. Wolves and their fans sought revenge. The Villa contingent wanted more of the same. Unfortunately, someone changed the script from the previous day's episode and, while the fans were treated to another seven goals, four of them were in Wolves' favour. Reg Chester scored two for Villa and Ronnie Dix hit one. 'Pongo' Waring summed it all up when he said, "We opened our presents on Christmas Day and then on Boxing Day we found that they didn't work!"

Since World War Two there have been many other exciting clashes between the major clubs of the Midlands, as Johnny Dixon recalls.

"Years ago we seemed to be playing derby games almost every week as there were several Midlands clubs at the top of the game. Every time we played Birmingham City you could guarantee that the ground would be packed and that it would be a very hard game. It was the same whenever we played against West Brom or Wolves. They had some great players like Billy Wright of Wolves and Ray Barlow of West Bromwich and those games were big occasions — especially if they were Cup-ties.

"Supporters looked forward to them and the players who were from the area would be especially involved. You couldn't help it! You were brought up to take sides even before you became a player. People talk about the derby games of Manchester and Liverpool and Glasgow, but the games in which we were involved against our Midlands rivals took some beating.

"I remember that we had something to prove when we played against Wolves on the day after Boxing Day in 1948. We had lost 3-0 at home to Birmingham earlier in December and then Wolves had beaten us 4-0 at Molineux on Christmas Day. I hadn't played in either of those games but I was in the side for the return with Wolves. There were 63,500 supporters in Villa Park that day and we were determined to do well. I think Wolves must have wondered what had hit them because they found the Villa side to be in a very different mood to the one they had beaten just two days earlier. Syd Howarth scored for us and Trevor Ford tore them apart with four goals — one was a penalty. The final score was 5-1 and the supporters celebrated as if we had just won the championship. It was a great day. To round it all off we beat Birmingham on the last day but one of the season at their place, so we finished with honours even!

"The following year we again played Wolves over Christmas, but this time the results were opposite. We beat them at Molineux and they beat us at Villa Park. We drew both games with Birmingham City but we had the edge over West Bromwich. We drew at the Hawthorns and then beat them at Villa Park.

"In the 1950-51 season I scored our first goal of the season — and that was in a derby match against West Bromwich on the opening day. We won 2-0 but they returned the compliment later in the season. We didn't play Birmingham that year but we did play Wolves and beat them both at home and away.

"I think the edge might have been taken off our local derby games because the Midlands teams kept changing divisions so much. We slipped out of the First Division for a while, as did Birmingham, West Bromwich and Wolves, so our derby games were not always annual occasions. I would like to see them all back in the Premiership now and I'm sure that when the teams met the excitement would be as great as ever it used to be."

Although Birmingham are the arch-rivals, some of the most thrilling games have been against West Bromwich. During Easter 1954, Villa and West Bromwich met on consecutive days. The first game was at the Hawthorns and resulted in a 1-1 draw — but the following day, Villa went on the rampage at their own ground and won 6-1.

"That was an amazing couple of days. More than 91,000 people saw the two games. Peter McParland's goal had earned us a draw on the Good Friday. The following day we were well prepared and we swamped them. Derek Pace and Joe Tyrrell scored two each, I got one and Danny Blanchflower also scored so we ran out 6-1 winners. We felt pretty good after that I can tell you!"

The sweet smell of success was permeated by some bitterness, however, when Wolves became champions at the end of the season.

The end of the 1955-56 season could not have been more dramatic for Villa. Their last game was at home to West Bromwich and, quite simply, they had to win to avoid relegation.

"Yes, I remember that game," said Johnny Dixon. "It was between us, Huddersfield and Sheffield United — and I think Preston were not exactly safe either. We knew that nothing less than a decent win over West Bromwich would do. I can't remember how goal average was worked out — it always seemed a bit complicated to me — but I knew that every goal would count on that last day.

"We won 3-0 with Les Smith scoring two goals and Len Millard of West Bromwich putting the ball into his own net. It was amazing because we finished just above Huddersfield who were relegated with the bottom club, Sheffield United. We finished on the same number of points as Huddersfield, but our goal average was just 0.2 better than theirs. I often wonder if that own-goal by Len Millard saved us from going down!"

The following season Villa rubbed salt in the West Bromwich wounds when they beat them in the FA Cup semi-finals and then went on to beat Manchester United at Wembley.

Alan Deakin spent most of his career at Villa Park and saw derby matches when he was still a schoolboy supporter.

"The atmosphere was fantastic. It was not just on matchday but for the whole week leading up to the game. You could talk to supporters of the opposition and have a bit of a banter between you. Then for the next few days after the game you would either go searching them out to gloat over them, or you would go into hiding yourself. They were always exciting games to watch. I don't ever remember one being just ordinary.

"Later, when you take part in the game as a player, they take on a whole new meaning. However, you never forget what it was like to be a supporter and that helps to fire you up even more because you know what it is like to see your side either win or lose on such an important occasion.

"One of the most memorable games against Birmingham City was one I missed. It was the League Cup Final of 1963 and both ourselves and City had made it through to the Final. I played in the first leg of the semi-final against Sunderland but I missed the second leg which was played more than three months later because the terrible weather which we were experiencing virtually froze out all football. The League programme was the same. By the time March came round we had played only two League games all year. Anyway, I had an injury problem and didn't play in the League Cup again that season, but I saw the games and, after losing 3-1 to City at St Andrew's, we threw everything at them in the return game. It ended goalless and so Birmingham won the Cup. That was hard to live with, especially since it was at the end of the season and there was no way we were going to be able to gain revenge until the following season."

Villa's championship season of 1980-81 saw them make almost a clean sweep of their derby games. They gained maximum points from all but one of their games against Birmingham, Coventry, West Bromwich and Wolves — a 0-0 draw at Albion spoiling what would otherwise have been a devastating blow to their local rivals. As it was, seeing Villa win the League title was probably devastating enough.

For Gary Shaw it was a magical season.

"There was only one thing I ever wanted to become when I was at school, and that was an Aston Villa player. I had always been a fan and remember going to Villa Park to see them play. I saw some great derby games and when it came to my turn to actually play in one I was really up for it. My first derby game was in the 1978-79 season. I had only played for a few minutes in one League game before that and that was three months earlier as a substitute.

"My first start to a League match was also my first derby game, away to West Bromwich. We drew 1-1 with Allan Evans scoring our goal. I would like to have finished on the winning side but, even so, I was more than happy to have played the full match and gone home with a point.

"Ron Saunders had told me not to try anything fancy, just to go out and enjoy myself. What a baptism though! A local derby in front of the TV cameras and 36,000 fans — including all my family and a lot of my friends. I was also playing against

John Wile and Alistair Robertson, two of the toughest and most experienced defenders in the First Division.

"I'll never forget the end of the game when Big John put his arm round my shoulders and told me that I'd had a good game and would go a long way. He knew that this had been my virtual first-team debut. It was a nice gesture from an opponent at the end of a cut and thrust derby game."

During Villa's championship season they played no fewer than eight derby games. Gary Shaw missed two of them but relished all the others.

"We won two championships that season, the League championship and the unofficial Midlands championship. We began our own series of derby games with a 1-0 win at Coventry. It was our fourth League game of the season. I had scored in two of the first three games but, when I scored the only goal of the game at Coventry, I could not stop laughing. I wasn't laughing at anyone — I was just thrilled to bits at scoring such an important goal in a derby match.

"I missed the next derby game at home to Wolves — which we won 2-1 — but a few weeks later we won 2-1 away to Birmingham City, Gordon Cowans getting the first with a penalty and Allan Evans the winner. I was in that game and, of all the derby possibilities, THE derby match is always against Birmingham City. It was all the more special to beat them on their own ground.

"We drew at West Bromwich 0-0. That was a tough game as I recall. The next match against local opposition was at home to Birmingham, yes, the return match. Just over 41,000 fans were at Villa Park and the atmosphere was brilliant. They were determined to get revenge for our win at St Andrew's, but we had lost at Middlesbrough the previous week and there was no way that Ron Saunders was going to let us lose two on the trot — especially when it was against Birmingham. I think he would have sacked the lot of us if we had lost!

"At the end of the game we had won 3-0. Dave Geddis scored two and the other scorer was a bloke called Shaw. Yes, me! After that we were set up for more victories over our local rivals. We beat Coventry 2-1, followed by a 1-0 win over Wolves and then, finally, a 1-0 away victory over West Bromwich. That last game was only the second one that I had missed all season — but what a season it was!"

Tony Daley is another local lad who watched many a derby game at Villa Park, not knowing that one day he would be taking part and having the roar of the crowd ringing in his ears, willing him to "put one over" on the neighbours.

"They're special matches aren't they?" he said. "When I was a lad we really used to look forward to the games against Birmingham and Wolves. If Villa won we couldn't wait to get to school on the Monday, just so that we could go around and make fun of the City or Wolves fans — not that there were too many of those at my school.

"When you join Villa, that enthusiasm doesn't wane, it actually gets stronger. Then when the time comes that you are playing for the first team you go into a different dimension. You are still a supporter at heart, but now you are a professional player with a job to do for your club.

"I remember the first time that I was in a League match against Birmingham. That was in September 1985. The day before I kept thinking, 'We're playing the City tomorrow — Wow!' I was quite wound up on the day of the game, but once we started I settled down and it became more like any other League match — although the supporters were even noisier than usual. The result was an anticlimax because we drew 0-0. I was disappointed really since, only a few days earlier, I had played in my first game against a local side when we beat West Bromwich 3-0 at the Hawthorns and I scored my first League goal. The return with City at Villa Park was a choker because they beat us 3-0. I try to forget that one!

"Because of being in different divisions I have not played against City very much. Since I joined Wolves I have wanted to be playing against Villa in Premiership matches, but the prospect of it actually happening one day is quite daunting. I still go to Villa Park and cheer on my old team but I would do my best to win if I was in a derby game against them. It would feel strange though after all these years of wanting the Villa to slaughter the local rivals."

Peter Withe is not a local lad, of course, having been born in Liverpool. His career took him to both Villa Park and St Andrew's, although it was his time in a Villa shirt which really earned him his fame. He has often said that being with Villa both as player and coach has been the icing on his career.

"I played for seven different League clubs during my career, but none more important to me than Villa. Before I joined in May 1980, I had had a season with Birmingham a few years earlier and, at St Andrew's, everyone wanted to beat Villa. When I came to Villa everyone wanted to beat Birmingham. It can make life a bit difficult, especially when you consider that I had also played for Wolves before I joined City. Although I come from Merseyside I knew what Midlands football was all about before I ever joined Villa. I think it is greatly under-estimated because there is as much passion in the Midlands as anywhere else in the country, and when Midlands sides are playing each other the atmosphere is as feverish as anywhere else on this planet.

"My first encounter between Villa and City was when I was playing for the Blues. We came to Villa Park in the 1975-76 season early on, and Villa won 2-1. Trevor Francis scored our goal. The return match was in the following April and this time we won 3-2. We were desperate for the points but we were also desperate to regain our pride. Andy Gray and Ray Graydon scored the Villa goals but Ken Burns, Terry Hibbitt and Trevor Francis got one each for City. I missed that game through injury but I was there to see it and it was a typical local derby with the tackles flying in and the crowd shouting themselves hoarse.

"My chance for glory against Birmingham came a few weeks into my first season in a Villa shirt. We played at St Andrew's and won 2-1. I was pleased with the result but I would have liked to have scored. Later in the season when we played the return at Villa Park, I was injured again and could not take part. Villa won 3-0 and that helped us on the way to the championship but I still had not scored a goal in a Villa-City derby match.

"The next season we were held at home by Birmingham in September 1981. It was a 0-0 draw, so another game without a goal for yours truly! My big moment came at last in the following February. We were playing the return game at St Andrew's and it looked as if we were heading for another goalless draw. Suddenly I found myself with a chance and I thought, 'I'm not going to let this one go'. Next thing the ball was in the net and I had broken my duck. It was the only goal of the game too, so I had a lot to celebrate when it was all over.

"I did not feel that I had been given the best of chances when I was with Birmingham so that goal meant a lot to me. I felt that I had proved myself against the team that I might still have been playing for. In October 1983 I again scored the only goal of the match against City, this time at Villa Park, and so during my time as an Aston Villa player I was more than happy with my personal contribution in the derby games. A few years later when I was playing for Sheffield United I had an eight-game loan period back with Birmingham City — however, I did not play in any of the derby matches against Villa. Just as well really!"

Stan Collymore has yet to play for Villa in a League match against Birmingham City but he would welcome the opportunity.

"I'd love to see all the Midlands clubs in the top division, not because of cutting down on travelling, but because I love the atmosphere of local derbies. I saw quite a few when I was a kid and they were always very special. Since I joined Villa the only local League derby games we have had were our two Premiership fixtures against Coventry. I was injured and missed the second game at Coventry although I was pleased that we won 2-1. I was delighted with the first one though — in December 1997 at Villa Park.

"I had not scored a League goal at all at Villa Park and the supporters were willing me to break my duck. We had been playing about 20 minutes when Mark Draper passed the ball to me and I sent it into the net from 25 yards. It was a great moment to see that net bulge. We went on to win 3-0 so my derby debut was complete.

"I should think that playing against Birmingham must be the ultimate for any Villa player. There is such a great tradition of rivalry between the two clubs that you automatically become a part of history."

Of course, it is not only in League matches that Villa have sparred with City, Wolves, West Bromwich and their other Midlands neighbours. However, Cup matches are a totally different story.

CHAPTER FOUR

THE
MANAGERS

SINCE the return of football in 1945, Aston Villa have had 18 managers up to and including John Gregory. The list includes some pretty famous names and a wide range of characters from the extrovert Ron Atkinson to the jovial Joe Mercer.

Alex Massie was in charge when the Football League was restarted, and he had the unenviable task of trying to pick up the pieces and give the fans back the Villa that had been so successful in the earlier part of the century. He had been a part of the pre-war Villa first-team squad, having joined the club from Hearts for £6,000 during a disastrous run in the 1935-36 season. His home debut did not stem the tide against Villa — in fact, it actually went into the soccer history books as Villa were beaten 7-1 by Arsenal and Ted Drake scored all seven of the Gunners' goals.

There were happier times ahead though and, before the war interrupted things, Alex Massie had endeared himself to the

Villa faithful and proved exactly why he was considered to be one of the best half-backs to come out of Scotland.

"When we won the Second Division championship at the end of the 1937-38 season we finally played as we knew we could," said Massie. "There were some fine players at Villa, Cummings, Philips and Griffiths among them, but we just did not play as a team and we were dismayed to be relegated in 1936. There were only a few points in it but for Aston Villa to be relegated was just not on. It took us two seasons but, in 1938, we were promoted as champions with Manchester United as runners-up."

Massie's appointment as manager came in August 1945 when he was still a player.

"I gave it some thought but it was an exciting challenge. Apparently it was offered to me as a reward for services rendered on the field. I tried to coach real football but I was probably adopting the wrong sort of tactics for what was needed at the time."

Those were philosophical words indeed. What Massie was trying to say was that he was trying to educate players while what was more likely to succeed was brute force. He kept Villa in the First Division but, in August 1950, he stood down because he felt that he had no more to offer the club. He became a football journalist in Birmingham for a while and then moved out of the area to coach at Welwyn Garden City.

Goalkeeper Alan Wakeman vividly recalls training sessions and matches with Massie in charge.

"He was a gentleman and a great player. He was tremendous in a game and never stopped encouraging everyone else as well as making sure that he gave total commitment himself. I suppose you would describe him as a cultured player.

He had real class and could do just about everything. If you needed a last-ditch tackle he would be there, but if you wanted a good brain and great accuracy in distributing the ball, he could do that too. He was a natural and I think that sometimes he found it hard to understand that others were not that good.

"As a manager he always wanted us to play good entertaining football. He would never hold with the kick-and-rush approach. I don't think that anyone could say that Aston Villa at that time played anything less than good football — but we were not always successful because other sides would adopt a more physical and direct approach. The supporters respected him otherwise he would have given up the job much earlier. In many ways he was probably ahead of his time."

After Alex Massie had departed just as the 1950-51 season was getting under way, there was a three-months gap before his replacement was appointed. The man chosen was George Martin who had previously been manager of Newcastle, whom he took to promotion in 1948. As a player he had been alongside the great Dixie Dean at Everton as well as playing with Hull, Middlesbrough and Luton. His playing career had begun with Hamilton Academical and, like Massie, Martin was a Scot.

It has to be said that Villa Park was not the happiest of places at the time.

"There seemed to be some disharmony behind the scenes, which made it very difficult for the managers and the players," said Harry Parkes. "I think the problem was that the directors of that era lacked forward thinking and, as a result, the club seemed to be going from month to month without any real sense of direction. Take that away and you begin to lose ambition and a club without ambition is always going to struggle. I'm sure that they all thought they were doing the right thing but what they probably needed was to step back and take a look at the over-all situation.

George Martin swept in as a new broom. What he found was a club at the crossroads. The players were concerned about their futures. To say that George Martin had walked into a pressure-cooker situation would be an understatement. The atmosphere inside the club was poor, but among the fans it was even worse. They could see Wolves and West Bromwich in the ascendancy while their own club was dithering. Nero's musical appreciation as flames licked around the amphitheatre springs to mind!

"It was a very difficult time for the manager," said Johnny Dixon. "There was a big black cloud hanging over the club and one man alone would find it very difficult to wave a magic wand and change everything. George Martin did his best but it just did not seem to work. We had some great times and some great results, but we seemed to be spending more time swimming against the tide rather than being carried along on the crest of a wave."

However it was not all bad news. Villa were turning into a "second half of the season" team, looking lost for the opening months and then staging a remarkable recovery to finish the season in a respectable position. In the 1951-52 season for example, Villa finished sixth in the First Division and only ten points behind champions, Manchester United. One point more and a slightly better goal average, and they would have been fourth and in line for a bonus payment.

The following season Villa once again started dismally with only two victories in the first ten games, but the big fight back in the second half of the season saw them finish in 11th place and reach the sixth round of the FA Cup.

"We just could not seem to settle at the start of the season. It was partly due to the fact that we had injuries to key players early on in each season while other clubs were at full strength," said former full-back Stan Lynn. "When we were finally able to get a settled side together the others were beginning to be troubled by injuries, so I think that had something to do with it."

With rivals Wolves and West Bromwich finally in much better positions in the First Division, the Villa supporters became more and more unhappy. The departure of a few star players did not help the situation either. Among those stars was Trevor Ford who was sold to Sunderland for, what was then, a British record fee of £30,000. The silver lining came in the form of Danny Blanchflower who was captured from Barnsley.

"He was an outstanding player and we probably did not realise at first what a gem George Martin had brought to Villa Park," said Johnny Dixon. "I think we paid £15,000 for Danny. Imagine that. A world-class player for £15,000!"

Another signing by Martin was Peter McParland who was spotted while playing for Dundalk in Irish football. His transfer fee was £3,880, another bargain, and McParland became a part of football folklore.

However, the signings, exciting though they were, did not in themselves signal the changes which were both hoped for and expected. In August 1953, Martin resigned.

The clamour that surrounded the departure of George Martin soon abated when Eric Houghton was appointed as manager.

"It was a good move because Eric had been so popular here as a player," said Johnny Dixon. "Eric Houghton *was* Aston Villa. The club definitely improved in many ways although we were still up and down the table. Eric was manager when we won the

FA Cup. He was a gentleman and the players wanted to do their best for him."

It was unfortunate that there had to be a series of player moves during Eric Houghton's reign because he probably never managed to get a really settled side together. Danny Blanchflower left for Tottenham, Tommy Thompson went to Preston and, while another five players were introduced, the brilliant form that was demonstrated in special occasion matches never manifested itself consistently enough for Villa to improve much on their constant battle against relegation.

Alan Deakin left school and became a junior during the Eric Houghton era.

"He was a lovely bloke who had Aston Villa engraved on his heart. You could see that the club meant everything to him. I was only a kid on the ground staff but he never ignored anyone and would always have a few words of encouragement for you. I was doing well in the youth team but I was not ready for the first team. He still used to encourage me and tell me that my time would come. I was grateful for that and told him so a few years later when he rejoined the club."

Eric Houghton tasted success with Villa's FA Cup win of 1957 but, despite finishing sixth at the end of the 1954-55 season, the great Villa revival did not really happen. As is usual it was the manager who bore the brunt of the criticism but in truth the problem was still that lack of ambition. The youth scheme was virtually non-existent, modernising the ground — including floodlights — was way down on the agenda, and even the prospect of entering the Fairs Cup by supplying players to a Birmingham representative team was greeted with all the enthusiasm engendered by a cold shower. Little wonder then that Villa Park was beginning to resemble a stagnant pond rather than the beautiful ornamental lake that had once been its centre-piece.

On a happier note, Eric Houghton did finally return to the club that he loved so much, first in an administrative capacity and then as a director — becoming the first vice-president of the club in 1983. He was renowned at Villa Park for being a most approachable man with a treasure-house of stories and a knowledge of the club that was unsurpassed.

Villa's next appointment was Joe Mercer, another of soccer's famous names who had earned the respect and love of soccer fans throughout the land in his playing days and who, as manager of Sheffield United, had demonstrated that he was more than capable of achievement as a boss. He arrived at Villa Park in December 1958. By that time the club's customary poor start was turning into a nightmare with only five victories gained from 21 matches. That might not sound like too much of a disaster until you look at some of the defeats — 7-2 at West Ham, 5-2 at Portsmouth, 4-0 at Wolves, 4-1 at home to West Brom, 6-3 at Leicester among them. Needless to say the defence was not just leaking goals but had allowed a flood! Joe Mercer had to make changes, among them giving Alan Deakin his debut.

"He was a great man, a really nice bloke, and that's not just because he gave me my chance in the first team. Everyone liked him. You would be hard pushed to find anyone who ever came into contact with him who would have a bad word to say about him. He was particularly good with the young players. Manchester United had their Busby Babes, but we became known as Mercer's Minors.

"My debut was against Middlesbrough in October 1959. We had been relegated the previous season and Joe Mercer's aim was to get us back into the First Division at the very first attempt. The supporters were behind him and so was everyone at the club. It hurt to go down and we were desperate to win promotion immediately. I got my chance when Vic Crowe was out. Bobby Thomson took Vic's No 4 shirt and I was given the No 8 shirt that Bobby normally wore. The boss told me not to worry about anything, keep my head and do my best. He was very reassuring. As it happens we won 1-0 with Stan Lynn getting the goal. There were nearly 35,000 people at Villa Park so it was a big occasion for me.

"I didn't play again that season because youth had to take second place to experience as the manager plotted our way to promotion. However, you were still made to feel a part of it and when we beat Charlton 11-1, I felt as excited as if I had been actually playing."

That result was part of a remarkable run of three great victories in a row. After Charlton's slaughter, Bristol City and Scunthorpe were then both beaten 5-0, which meant that in the three games Villa had scored a total of 21 goals with only one in reply. Gerry Hitchens was having a field day with five against Charlton, three against Bristol City and two against Scunthorpe.

Joe Mercer achieved his goal and Villa were promoted as champions of the Second Division. Suddenly the club was on the right track.

"The mood had changed considerably," said Alan Deakin. "We felt confident. I was involved with the first team nearly all the time and in our first season back in Division One, 1960-61, I began to get regular games and it proved to be a good season for us. We finished ninth in the First Division and won the very first League Cup.

"It has to be said that the changes in our fortunes were really all down to Joe Mercer. He signed the right people and whether he was coaching, explaining tactics, or just having a few words with an individual player, he was always firm but gentlemanly. The players trusted him. If Joe Mercer said that you should play a certain way, you never questioned him. You just knew that he would be right!"

There was some financial improvement for the club in the early part of the Mercer era. In 1960 the club reported a loss of £16,000. A year later there was a profit of £19,651. Joe Mercer's youth policy was already beginning to produce the goods and, during his time in the Villa hot-seat, he saw Charlie Aitken, Alan Deakin, Alan Baker, John Sleeuwenhoek, Mike Tindall and Mick Wright among those who began their careers under his guidance.

Consternation followed congratulation when Villa began to slip again. The truth eventually came out that Joe Mercer was unwell. In the latter part of the 1963-64 season he was forced to rest and, just when he seemed to be well on the way to recovery, he and Villa parted company. Did he jump, or was he pushed? Today it doesn't matter very much but it was the subject of much speculation when it happened. Depending upon which particular newspaper you happened to be reading, Mercer was either sacked, resigned, or amicably left by mutual agreement. The truth? We shall probably never really know, but general opinion is that the situation could have been handled in a much more dignified manner. To the end Joe Mercer refused to discuss the matter, simply saying, "Apart from the last season and a half, which were difficult for various reasons, I had a very happy time with Aston Villa!"

Villa supporters were not at all happy at what they saw as a disappointing and unseemly decision. Mercer had been unwell for some time, stress being blamed for his ill-health. They were annoyed that he had been supposedly sacked just as he was on the road to recovery. He had endeared himself to them by masterminding the resurgence of Villa and by structuring a youth policy to safeguard the future of the club by developing home-grown talent.

The choppy waters were calmed a little when Dick Taylor was immediately appointed as Mercer's replacement in July 1964. Taylor had been Mercer's assistant throughout his time at Villa Park and had taken charge of team affairs during his enforced absence. Not only that but Taylor was a West Midlands local having been born and bred in Wolverhampton. Once again the Villa board had pulled off a public relations master-stroke.

"I think it was expected that nothing would really change but it's only natural that any manager would want to put his own ideas into operation," said Alan Deakin. "Dick Taylor made a few changes to our players' style but one of the major problems was another round of changing faces. We still could not get a settled side and confidence was up and down all the time."

Dick Taylor was busy in the transfer market and during his time in charge he produced a profit in financial terms but a deficit in progress. For two seasons the club struggled to finish 16th in the table, but then disaster struck in the 1966-67 season when Villa slumped to 21st and were subsequently relegated to Division Two. The biggest problem seemed to be in a defence which conceded 85 goals in 42 League matches.

Colin Withers was in goal for most of that season, but he is still at a loss to be able to explain exactly what went wrong.

"On paper we had a strong defence. The individual players

were certainly good enough but there was probably something lacking in confidence and teamwork. Whatever, it was a miserable season all round for everyone involved. I felt sorry for the supporters. They had backed us all the way and it had all been in vain."

Blackpool had finished in the bottom spot but Villa were four points adrift of safety, and there was no consolation in the fact that Southampton — in 19th place — had actually conceded seven more goals than Villa. When you are relegated, consolation ceases to be a factor! The bad news was made worse by the promotion of Midlands rivals Wolves and Coventry from the Second Division.

The inevitable happened, of course, and Dick Taylor, his assistant Johnny Dixon and chief scout Jimmy Easson were all dismissed. Dignity prevailed but Taylor did have one parting shot when he said, "I think Villa have got to get around and find out more about what's going on at other clubs."

He was referring to the wage structure. The club was still living in the past in his opinion and quality players had been lost because Villa would not keep in touch with modern salary requirements. He warned that the club was in danger of losing its status as one of the major teams in the country. His words had an ominous ring.

Tommy Cummings was appointed as the new manager in July 1967 and could not conceal his excitement at the prospect of taking over at Villa Park.

"To say that I am excited and in a whirl at the turn of events would be an understatement," he said at the time. He probably could not have taken over the manager's seat at a worse moment. The morale within the club was lower than low, the supporters were totally fed-up, and the local media — staunch allies for years — had finally begun to reflect the voice of the fans and seemed to reach campaign proportions in their attacks on the Villa board. This was not a good time to be trying to get comfortable in the hot-seat of a club already at boiling point.

There were additions to the board but the upheaval continued, and from one day to the next nobody knew exactly what the latest developments would be. It is difficult to motivate players who are constantly distracted by the musical chair activities of their bosses. The upshot was yet another miserable season in which relegation was staved off, but not by very much. The 54 goals scored duplicated the number scored the previous season and added up to a lack of firepower. Fans are by nature forgiving optimists, but deny them goals and hell hath no fury like them. They stayed away in their droves and those that did attend stood mainly in silent disbelief, or booed their feelings at the end of a game. It was all summed up in the last game of that highly forgettable season when Villa were at home to Queen's Park Rangers and lost 2-1. It was an own-goal by Villa's Keith Bradley which settled the game and epitomised Villa's situation.

The following season began as the previous one had finished. The first 20 games yielded only 16 goals, one of which was an own-goal and three others penalties. That own-goal had actually been very precious because it had resulted in one of the three victories gained at that stage. Boiling point had been reached and now the cauldron was overflowing. Cummings and his assistant Malcolm Musgrove were dismissed.

"I feel that I can leave Villa Park secure in the knowledge that the foundation of the new Villa, in the shape of the youth scheme, has been laid, and that my twelve months' work as manager have not been wasted," said Cummings. Later he added, "It was probably a hopeless task from the start. The club was in a bad way and no manager can be successful at a time like that. Perhaps at a different time it might have been an altogether different outcome — but that we shall never know. I do not regret my time at Villa. It is a fine club, always has been, but, unfortunately, it just went through a patch of illness."

Arthur Cox was caretaker manager for just a few weeks and it was during his spell that matters really came to a head. The board resigned and a new board took over, headed by Doug Ellis and including Harry Parkes, the former Villa favourite. They took immediate decisive action and appointed a new manager — a man with a reputation both as a player and as a coach and manager. Tommy Docherty was that man.

Docherty has never been short of words. He is one of the most quoted British football characters of all time, perhaps surpassed only by Bill Shankly. When he arrived at Villa he said, "I'd love to stay at Villa Park for the rest of my career, but in football who can tell?" It proved to be an almost prophetic statement because the Doc remained in surgery at the club for no more than 13 months before patience ran out — but what a time that was!

"He came in like a whirlwind," said Alan Deakin. "He had a reputation for being a hard taskmaster, and he was. He also had a reputation for having a sense of humour and he had that too. He woke everyone up but possibly his character was just a little too unsettling at times."

Docherty produced new players and results. To be fair, the club looked doomed to another relegation before he arrived but, in a magical run after he had taken over after Tommy Cummings, the side suffered only four more defeats and, from a seemingly hopeless position at the bottom of the table, they climbed back to the safety of 18th. A run in the FA Cup to the fifth round helped and a crowd of 59,084 turned up to witness the fourth replay at home, proving that even if the fortunes of the club had not been much for some years, the potential was still there.

There were celebrations at the end of the season and a huge wave of optimism that Villa would be promoted at the conclusion of the 1969-70 season. The squad went to Atlanta for six weeks to prepare for the new season and, at the same time, there were new faces arriving — among them Bruce Rioch from Luton.

"It was quite an experience to play for Tommy Docherty. I played for him again later at Derby County, but that was different. To be quite honest, I think Docherty was the victim of circumstances with his only real mistake being to forsake his own character and gut feelings for a short time.

"By nature he was a hard man and a ruthless manager. I am sure that he wanted to make changes to the squad during that summer and dispose of some of the players he had inherited. The trouble was that he uncharacteristically let his heart rule his head and decided to keep them all. He appreciated the fact that they had all worked hard for him during the latter part of the previous season and he wanted to give them the chance to continue — even though he knew that they should have been replaced. It was never his way to allow sentiment to enter into his style of management — but on this occasion he did!

"The expectation and optimism which had built up as the start of the new season dawned was electrifying. However, there was still upheaval behind the scenes. The club had been in free-fall when Docherty took over as manager. The new board of directors was trying to get things back on an even keel, but they had a lot of work to do. It was almost like a club which had gone into liquidation and was starting all over again. There was a new share issue to raise some capital and a number of wounds that had to be healed. It was not just up to the board. As manager, Tommy Docherty was involved in the surgery that the club required. At the same time he had a group of players who had to be motivated and turned into a promotion-winning squad.

"Having brought in three or four new players during the summer — younger players like myself — a few of the older players were none too happy about their situation and there was some disharmony in the dressing-room. I got on well with Tommy. I was a 21-year-old who did just exactly what he was told. I had no axe to grind and every day was marvellous as far as I was concerned. I had even enjoyed seeing the ground developments, but some of the senior players who had been at Villa Park did not share my enthusiasm. Had Tommy followed his original instinct and replaced some of those players instead of adding to them, I think there might have been a different story.

"In addition, our training facilities were poor. There used to be a training ground for the club but the previous board had sold it and we were training at different places all the time — sometimes even in a local park if nowhere private was available. Later of course, the club acquired Bodymoor, but at this stage our facilities were little better than for a local pub team. Tommy had a good coaching team in Arthur Cox, Graham Leggat, Peter Doherty, and Vic Crowe, who had given up his post with Atlanta to take over the Villa reserves. Even with all their experience and talents, however, they didn't have a single magic wand between them.

"Our first fixture of the season finally arrived and 32,663 turned up at Villa Park to watch us play Norwich. We lost 1-0 with Ken Foggo scoring the Norwich goal. It was a big disappointment and it became worse as we drew two and lost seven of our first nine games. The mood behind the scenes grew worse and it became obvious that something would have to give."

By mid-November Villa were 21st in the Second Division with the unthinkable once again becoming a real issue. Docherty had already used 27 players in the first team and, as the Reserves and youth side were faring just as badly, Villa Park took on the look of a hospital waiting room with the unwell mingling with the anxious visitors. Club discipline also suffered and there was a public row when Dick Edwards, Mike Ferguson and Barrie Hole were each fined £10 for drinking in a pub two nights before a match. Tommy Docherty had dug in though.

"I have not lost my confidence in my ability," he said. "We are having enough of the play in matches but simply can't get the ball into the net."

Bruce Rioch, meanwhile, was one of the first names on the team sheet for every game.

"We kept reading the word 'crisis' in the newspapers but were assured that there was no crisis. It was just a bad patch which would pass once we could string a few decent results together. Matters came to a head in the middle of January. We were at home to Portsmouth with just over 21,000 at Villa Park. We scored three goals, of which I got two, but Portsmouth scored five! A 5-3 home defeat was just about the last straw."

Doug Ellis issued a statement which said that any speculation about the manager's imminent departure was unfounded. Docherty went on record as saying, "I'm still sure that I can get the club out of trouble." However, two days after the Portsmouth game, there was a prolonged board meeting at the club and the gathered press were told that Tommy Docherty was no longer manager of Aston Villa. Docherty had little to say as he left except to express his disappointment that he had not been given more time to turn the corner. In fairness he was probably right. The Doc had not just been asked to perform surgery, he had been expected to be a miracle worker.

"He inherited a good football club at the wrong time," said Bruce Rioch. "The club needed time and surgery. If he had followed his instincts in the summer and discarded the players that he wanted to discard he would have had a better chance. If you upset a few senior players you have an uphill struggle. Either they go or you go. Tommy tried to be fair and it backfired badly. I think he was very unlucky."

Vic Crowe was immediately appointed to take over from Docherty and in his first press statement he paid a back-handed compliment to the former boss when he said, "We *must* stay in the Second Division. I pray that I can do the same as Tommy did in his first three months here."

Vic Crowe was not alone in his prayers!

CHAPTER FIVE

AND MORE MANAGERS

TOMMY Docherty was gone but Vic Crowe remained. Vic had given up a good coaching post in the USA to join Villa as assistant to The Doc. Now he found himself in charge. He was a popular choice with the fans who remembered him as an uncompromising midfielder and captain of the Villa side during the early 1960s — a players' player who had become a Welsh international. The players respected him for his attitude and his record which meant that everyone was happy. But could he deliver? Bruce Rioch was there at the time.

"Vic was very good with the players. He did not hide the enormity of the task that lay ahead and he did not make any rash promises. He expected everyone to do their best and sent us out in a positive frame of mind. He had a great ally in Ron Wylie, who joined as his assistant, and they made a great managerial team. We were relegated at the end of the season. Things had gone just too far by the time Vic took over, but he was building for the future virtually from the word 'go'. It was

Vic Crowe who instigated the new training ground, Bodymoor. We had been training just about anywhere and that hadn't helped our cause at all. We did the best we could to keep Villa in the Second Division but when the season ended we were in 21st place with only Preston beneath us. We both went down into the Third Division — unknown territory for Aston Villa."

Ironically, Villa's worst season to date was rewarded by their best average home attendances for seven years — proof indeed that the fans were prepared to stretch their loyalty to the full.

"Vic disposed of a few players and I suspect that they were the same players that Tommy Docherty would have let go if he had been his usual self. During the summer Vic basically turned the club around. He knew that there would have to be a fresh start if Villa were going to get back up the League."

From Portugal, where he had landed a job with Oporto, Tommy Docherty was watching the developments and said, "I did not admit it at the time but it broke my heart to leave Villa. I am still a shareholder and if ever I am in a position to support a club it will be Aston Villa. I was never happier than during my days at Villa Park."

He added, "If I had not been sacked the team would have been out of trouble weeks before the end of the season."

We shall, of course, never know if that would have been true; what we do know is that the Crowe-Wylie management team did prove to be the cure for Villa's sickness.

"They were tremendous and we were very confident as we approached the new season," said Bruce Rioch. "I had got on well with Tommy but I got on equally well with Vic and Ron. I always considered myself to be a small fish in a big pond and listened to what they said. I was keen to learn and could not have had better tutors."

Villa launched spiritedly into the new season. The first game was a League Cup match at home to Notts County. It resulted in a 4-0 victory and was the very first step on the road to Wembley as Villa were later to play against Tottenham in the Final. The Division Three campaign also started with a victory, a 3-2 success at Chesterfield. Pat McMahon scored Villa's first League goal of the season and Bruce Rioch scored the next two. With only two defeats in the first 15 games, Villa were obviously the team to beat. Their opponents had an extra incentive to keep them in the Third Division because wherever they played, at home or away, the crowds flocked to see them.

Promotion was the target but somehow it eluded them.

"We had one or two odd results and I think they did the damage. We finished fourth in the table and that just wasn't good enough. It was particularly annoying to see Preston, the team with whom we had been relegated, going straight back up as champions. There was no panic though. Vic and Ron kept their heads and made sure that we kept ours. They were dedicated to getting us back to the top and made sure that we did not lose sight of our target either. There was the consolation of getting to Wembley in the League Cup Final, but it was promotion that we really wanted — especially for the Villa supporters who had been absolutely marvellous.

"The following season we got off to a good start again. A few further adjustments had been made to the squad but basically it was more of the same as we built on the progress of the previous season. By May we had won the Third Division and we were at last on the way back. It was all credit to Vic Crowe and Ron Wylie who had halted the slide and given Villa back its pride."

They did not stop there, of course. Vic Crowe had vowed to

get the club back to the top and, while he was delighted to have conquered the Third Division, his eyes fell immediately on the next target of promotion from the Second Division.

The 1972-73 season started well enough with seven wins and only one defeat in the first ten games. Then came a small slump followed by inconsistency so that, by the time Villa hit a silver streak at the end of the campaign, promotion proved to be just a little bit out of reach. Finishing third was a creditable performance but meant that Villa were confined to Second Division football for yet another season.

On 25 August 1973, the Villa fans turned up to see the first game of the new season. A goal each from Charlie Aitken and Trevor Hockey sent them home happy at the end of a 2-0 defeat of Preston. First Division here we come — or so it seemed! In fact Villa slumped again. Two defeats by West Bromwich rubbed salt into the wounds and when the club finished in 14th place, pangs of relegation having been in the stomach, there was going to be only one conclusion.

What happened next was to prove to be a major turning point in the history of Aston Villa. It can be summed up in two words — Ron Saunders! It may have seemed like yet another gamble when Saunders was appointed in June 1974 because he had just been sacked by Manchester City after only five months in charge. His "crime" had been getting City to the League Cup Final and not winning it. Prior to that he had enjoyed a very successful managerial career with Yeovil, Oxford and Norwich.

Brian Clough had been mentioned as the possible new manager, and Cloughie was definitely interested.

"Any manager would want to take on such a job with a club like Aston Villa," he said. "It is a big club, a club that should always be among the championship chasers. I would probably have taken up the post there if I had been approached — but nobody asked me."

The supporters definitely wanted him. His insistence, publicly, that the club contact him, rather than the other way about, proved to be a point too far for Doug Ellis who immediately struck Clough's name off the list of possibles. Yes, it had to be Ron Saunders.

"I asked a lot of questions when I arrived," said Saunders. "I wanted to learn as much about the club as possible, not just the current players but the club itself, where it had been, what it had been doing, and where it thought it was going next. I have never been a great one for talking big to the press, so there were no dramatic promises."

Of course, Ron Saunders has since become synonymous with Aston Villa's greatest post-war period — so far! The journey, however, was not entirely smooth. Saunders, understandably, wanted to stamp his own mark on the club and its methods and tactics, which meant that some of the established names would quickly have to become accustomed to a different style — and in some cases, different jobs. The decisions that Saunders took did not please everybody, but he carried out his task regardless of sentiment or protest.

"In his shoes I would have done the same thing," said Bruce Rioch. "A manager carries the can from all sides so he might as well do what he thinks is best and stand or fall by the consequences. Ron Saunders did what he thought was the right thing for Aston Villa at that time. I don't think that anyone could say that he was wrong to make such changes because the results prove him right whichever way you look at them."

Saunders had always been his own man and could not do the job in any other way than by his own self-assertion.

"The situation at Aston Villa did not lend itself to be able to wave a magic wand," he said. "There was no money available for an influx of new players, so it was a case of having to make do with what we had. During that first season my major signing was Frank Carrodus from Manchester City — but we did not break the bank for him. The way we were placed we had to make sure that the players had two major assets — super-fitness and self-belief! Those were the things that we worked on mostly. The side was reasonably balanced with a good cross-section of players for the various positions. I signed Carrodus to increase our options just a little and there were some young players coming through that I thought would be worth a try. That was how it was during that first season, we just had to do our best."

As the season unfolded, the optimism increased at Villa Park, and not just in the League either as goalkeeper Jim Cumbes recalls.

"We drew the first three matches 1-1, which meant that we were soon in the lower half of the table. The fact that we were also unbeaten meant little to Ron Saunders. We knew that nothing less than victory would get us promotion and he was determined that we would get the results we needed. I missed our fourth game through injury and we won 6-0. I was delighted but a little worried that my place in the side could be threatened. I missed four games in all but once I was back I stayed there for the rest of the season. The thing I remember mostly about Ron Saunders, apart from his obvious brilliance as a manager, was that you rarely saw him smile very much. I think everyone was frightened of him really. It's not that he never smiled, just not very often! When we made progress in the League we also made progress in the League Cup and I think the good results in one helped to encourage us in the other."

Ron Saunders believes that it was the League Cup which

inspired Villa to one of the best run-ins to a season ever seen at Villa Park.

"I think getting to the League Cup Final at Wembley made all the difference. We beat my old club, Norwich, and after that our Division Two form was tremendous. We lost only one game from the League Cup Final to the end of the season. It set us up beautifully for promotion as Division Two runners-up to Manchester United."

The League Cup Final win over Norwich was on 1 March 1975 and, indeed, in the remaining twelve Second Division games Villa lost one, drew one and won all the others.

During the next few seasons Ron Saunders continued to make changes among his playing staff. Some famous faces left, while others arrived to become famous. The manager was working on a jigsaw puzzle that would ultimately make Aston Villa the top club in the country.

Gary Shaw, like most of the Villa players, had a very healthy respect for his boss.

"He was a difficult man to please. Not too much praise came my way from him but I got used to that and never really expected any. It was just his way. There's no denying that he was good at his job and we all respected him for that."

Tony Morley was also there during the reign of Ron Saunders.

"Ron was a very, very hard man. If you did the business he would look after you. If you didn't you knew what to expect. He would give you three or four games to get your form together. If you didn't take that chance then you were out. Everyone knew that was how he worked and so there were no big mistakes. There was no sentiment in his decisions and he was right. This is a profession and you sink or swim on your performances."

After several seasons of unfulfilled championship potential, Villa had only the success in the 1977 League Cup to keep them going. However, all that was about to change when the 1980-81 season dawned. In many ways it was a patchy season with some good runs and some not-so-good runs. That self-belief prevailed though and any confidence crisis was quickly brushed aside. The championship went to the last game of the season and, even though Villa lost at Arsenal, their rivals, Ipswich, were also beaten and when they caught the coach back to the Midlands, Villa did so as champions. Ron Saunders and his men were feted for weeks, and rightly so!

The following season was to be one of the most exciting yet most puzzling in the club's wonderful history. Fantastic progress was made in Europe but on the domestic front the club was struggling. Within a few weeks Villa were in the relegation zone and stayed there. By March the emotions were totally schizophrenic, with Europe producing euphoria and the First Division results creating despair. Then came the shock as Ron Saunders resigned.

Peter Withe recalled receiving the news.

"We were all really shocked. We had not even considered such a thing. It really surprised me since I had joined on the strength of my conversations with Ron Saunders. With what we had achieved so far it really was a big surprise. We all felt that we were going places and that our League situation was curable. We were stunned."

Villa asked Tony Barton, Ron's assistant, to take over as caretaker until they made an official appointment. Within a few weeks, on 1 April 1982, the board announced their decision — Tony Barton was now to be the new manager on a permanent basis.

"Tony didn't make any great changes when he took over," said Peter Withe. "We were on course for Europe and that probably became our major target — although that doesn't mean we didn't try our hardest in the League. I think that if a completely new manager had been appointed it could have been a disaster. He would have had to make changes and that could have disrupted everything. We were all pleased for Tony and we had confidence in him."

Tony Barton, quite deliberately, did not make any changes.

"I didn't see any point. It was all going quite well. We had allowed some silly results in the League so we had to tighten up a little in those games, but there was no reason for anyone to panic. The teams I sent out were little different from those that Ron had picked earlier in the season."

Results in the League did improve and Villa finished in mid-table — an unexciting but secure position, which meant that they could cast off any domestic worries and enjoy themselves in the European Cup Final in Rotterdam. And enjoy themselves they did — at the expense of Bayern Munich.

"The season ended with everyone on the crest of a wave," declared Tony Barton. "It was a credit to the players that they had achieved so much, but it was also a great tribute to Ron Saunders who had done so much to put Villa on the way to becoming the top side in Europe."

They say that a footballer or a manager is only as good as his last result. That is probably quite true in general. Villains and heroes regularly swap roles, depending upon their most recent performance. Tony Barton went from being a hero, to being a 'nice man', to being a villain as the following seasons failed to yield anything in the way of silverware. The supporters were upset, reluctantly, but worse, the board was upset and not just by the mediocrity on the pitch. There was yet another financial crisis and this stifled Barton's chances of buying top new faces to inspire his side. He had to sell to buy and, as so often happens in those cases, the whole objective was defeated before it started. In June 1984, Tony Barton's services were no longer required. He was replaced by Graham Turner.

"I saw the need to make major changes and so I did," said Turner. He certainly did. One by one the familiar faces disappeared. Some were disappointed, but for others the Turner era was a masterpiece to be admired.

"You won't hear me complaining," explained Tony Daley. "I made my first-team debut thanks to Graham Turner. He picked me to play away to Southampton in April 1985. We lost 2-0 but I played in four more First Division games that season and it launched my career. The following season he picked me quite regularly and helped my confidence all the time. For me he was a good manager and he would probably have been more successful at a different time. The club was going through a funny stage in its life, with things going on behind the scenes and football itself in a bit of a depression because of the crowd problems in the Heysel Stadium and the fire at Bradford. It was all very unsettling for everyone."

In September 1986 the inevitable happened. Villa had made a terrible start to the season with six defeats in the first seven games, including a 6-0 hammering by Nottingham Forest — managed of course by the coveted Brian Clough. Villa were already in the relegation zone and supporters were wise enough to know that unless something drastic happened, the club was destined to go down once again. For many it was more than they could stand and home attendances slumped by about 10,000 a game.

After Graham Turner left, the board made a rather bizarre appointment in Billy McNeill. It was not that McNeill was bizarre. In fact he was a hero, having been one of the celebrated 'Lisbon Lions' as a player and later managing both Celtic and Manchester City to great success. However, it seemed to be an odd signing for Villa and an even stranger post for McNeill to take up when he could virtually have written his own contract anywhere in Scotland. In fact he did later go back to have further discussions with Celtic after his contract with Villa ended.

"It was the challenge, there's no doubt about that," said McNeill. "I saw a sleeping giant and I had to try and wake it up. I could not understand why Villa were not winning trophies every season. A big club like that needed success, yet here it was struggling against another decline into a lower division. The opportunity came for me to try and do something — so I did. It didn't work out though. I tried all sorts of things but the self-destruct button had already been pushed and, even though there were a few encouraging results, it was too late. Looking back it was certainly an experience, but probably a mistake nonetheless."

In the last few weeks of the season Villa lost each of their remaining three games. They finished at the bottom of Division One, were relegated, and once again found themselves in need of a new manager.

The choice of manager in July 1987 was an inspired one as Graham Taylor slid into the hot-seat. Taylor recognised the enormity of the task and was excited by the challenge.

"I have been at Watford for ten years and we had a terrific time together, but I could not resist the challenge of coming to Aston Villa. This is completely different to what I have experienced at Vicarage Road. Here at Villa Park we have a genuinely big club, one of the biggest in Britain, in decline. Not only do we have to arrest that decline but we have to get the club back to where it belongs as quickly as possible."

Later he admitted that the club was probably in an even worse state than he had realised, but he paid tribute to those who were there at the time.

"The players responded really well and so did all the back-room staff. We knew we had a mighty task but we were united in the effort and, with the supporters backing us all the way, we did manage to turn the whole thing round."

The Taylor era did not start in a terribly auspicious fashion with only one victory in the first seven League matches. To rub salt into the wound, one of the defeats was at home to Birmingham City who were comfortable 2-0 victors. Then came another local derby in the eighth game of the season, away to West Bromwich, and that proved to be the turning point.

"We won 2-0 with Warren Aspinall scoring both goals, and that seemed to be a major turning point," said Taylor. "I think we only lost one other game in the next five months."

It was quite true and Villa even gained revenge over Birmingham with a 2-1 win at St Andrew's. There were other defeats in the later stages of the season but Villa still managed to keep up with the leaders of the Second Division.

"We thought that we might make the play-offs, but nobody expected that we would finish with an automatic promotion place," Graham Taylor recalls. "It all happened on the last day of the season when we drew at Swindon. Millwall finished as champions of the division and Middlesbrough and ourselves finished on level points. We had scored five more goals than them and that was enough to see us given second place and automatic promotion. There had been so many possibilities and permutations flying about that we took a long, hard look at all the mathematics before we started celebrating.

"When it had finally sunk in that we were back in the top division at the first attempt we were all delighted. For me it was very special because I knew what it meant to the club and its supporters. It meant a lot to me too. I had grown up in the knowledge that Aston Villa was one of the really big clubs and now we had managed to get this fallen giant back on its feet."

The next two seasons saw Villa continue to make progress. Their first season back in Division One was a struggle at times but, by the end of the it, they finished in 17th place and had survived that all-important first season of rehabilitation. A 7-0 hammering of Birmingham City in the two legs of a League Cup-tie certainly gave the Villa fans something to savour too.

"There was still a lot of rebuilding going on so we were not expecting to win anything in that first season back at the top," said Taylor, who changed the majority of players during his few years. "I was just thrilled that we were there and that we stayed there. Taylor was responsible for bringing in players like David Platt, Dwight Yorke and Paul McGrath. He was also a great source of encouragement to Tony Daley.

"I know Graham Taylor has had his fair share of stick over the years, but he was brilliant for me. Of all the managers I played for at Villa, Graham Taylor probably did the most for my career. He took a personal interest in my progress and helped me to play my own game within the requirements of the side. He also picked me for internationals when he became England manager, and I feel that I owe him a lot for the part that he has played in my career."

In the 1989-90 season Villa were once again a different side.

Possibly they could even have been champions. Liverpool finished top of the League that season but Villa were not too far behind in second place — and when the two clubs met the result was a 1-1 draw both at home and away. There was a fairly wide gap between Liverpool and Villa, but equally there was a wide gap between Villa and Tottenham in third place. The prospects looked extremely good for the 1990-91 season, but Villa were to go into it without Graham Taylor who had taken up the offer of becoming manager of England.

"I would not have left Aston Villa for any other position. I was very happy there and it was frustrating to leave when there was still a job to do. We had already done quite a bit of the journey but there was still the final lap to achieve. I am sure we would have gone on to win the championship during the next season or two but I just could not turn down the England job. I don't think anyone could walk away from the honour of being manager of their country — I'm sure I couldn't!"

Nobody blamed Taylor for leaving Villa. He had done well during his time there and had given back some of the lost pride and optimism. Dwight Yorke also recalled the major part that Taylor played in his career.

"I shall always appreciate what Graham Taylor did for me. He took a chance on a teenage kid and certainly made sure, when I was so far away from home, that I was taken care of and not just left to get homesick. He was very encouraging all the time and gave me a great grounding in my first year in this country."

While Taylor settled into his new job as an international manager, a former international manager settled into his new job at Villa Park. Josef Venglos was a name known to few in Britain, but he had just steered Czechoslovakia to the quarter-finals of the World Cup in Italy. It was a tribute to the business acumen and ambition of Villa chairman, Doug Ellis, that he had managed to secure the services of a coach who had such a high profile on the continent — even though little-known here.

Venglos had a hard act to follow. Taylor had been voted "Manager of the Month" on three consecutive occasions, and had endeared himself to the Villa faithful. As always, they were more than happy to welcome the new man and give him the chance to show what he could do. Venglos had no real fears about taking up the challenge in what had been described to him as "the toughest League in the world".

"Of course there will be pressures. I have experienced this in international football all over the world. When I was manager of Slovan Bratislava I was expected to win the championship every season. At Sporting Lisbon the directors expected me to get the club into Europe every season. Now that I have achieved my ambition of coming into English football, I want Villa to be winning too!"

The sentiment was right, but this was not to be his most memorable season. Villa's form was totally inconsistent. The mood went out of the camp and what should have been a season of celebration became instead a campaign of crumbling confidence as Villa went out of Europe — following that failure by a run of League form which saw only two victories in fourteen games. Once again there were fingers hovering over the panic button, and the well-meaning supporters found it increasingly difficult to enthuse over what had become inept performances, not helped by a series of injury problems. What had really gone wrong? Tony Daley has a simple answer.

"I think he was just ahead of his time in many ways. He was a master tactician and he came with a proven record, but there were language difficulties at times and I don't think he was always able to express himself exactly in the way that he wanted. Perhaps today it might have been different with interpreters and language tuition playing such an important part in the game. I also think that his style of play would have been much more successful in the latter part of the 1990s than they were at the beginning of the decade. In some ways I felt sorry for him. He was quite a nice man and did want to be successful here, but things just did not go right for him."

There is no argument with that. Villa finished in 17th place and suffered three defeats late in the season which did not help their cause at all, since Arsenal, Manchester City and Leeds, all put five goals past them during those latter weeks.

Another tough decision had to be made and Josef Venglos was on his way. Who could Villa turn to as their new saviour? It would have to be someone with a pretty spectacular image. In other words it just had to be Ron Atkinson, a former Villa player and a man with whom the fans could identify, and for whom the players would be prepared to give their all.

Amid quite a furore, Ron walked away from Sheffield Wednesday, where he had turned the club's fortunes around, and took up the gauntlet at Villa Park. If nothing else it was an easier journey for him since his home had been in Birmingham for a number of years.

"I have always loved Aston Villa. I still do. When the chance to become manager occurred I was really torn in two. Sheffield Wednesday meant a lot to me. In a short time we had travelled far together. I did not want to leave Wednesday but neither did I want to turn Villa down. It was a very difficult situation. In the end my love and desire to achieve something with Villa won the day and I just had to take up their offer.

"The challenge was great. Graham Taylor had been successful and there was the anticipation of great times ahead and a return to winning the championship. My job was to restore confidence and build a side that could finish the job and take the title back to Villa Park."

He nearly did too. Eyebrows were raised when he put Dalian Atkinson and Cyrille Regis into Villa shirts — but it worked! Ironically, his first League match was against Sheffield Wednesday, an acrimonious fixture at the end of which Ron was happy to have completed and also won 3-2. It is always good to record a win from your first game of the season, especially an away match, but somehow that victory also asserted Ron's arrival at Villa Park.

"I had been an amateur player at Villa, but I was a fan even before that, having been brought up in Birmingham. It would have been nice to have made the grade as a professional player at the club but it was not to be. In truth I did not play one first-team game so I was very keen to make up for that when I became manager. I was very hungry to win trophies with the club."

Jim Barron remembers Atkinson as a player.

"He hasn't changed a bit from those early days. He was big, brash and as mad about football then as he is now. If anything, he became a better player once he started on his management career."

At Villa Park the arrival of Big Ron was reminiscent of the appointment of Tommy Docherty. Both were charismatic characters and both were instant successes with the Villa fans. Ron's first Premiership game in charge had been a success, but could he sustain and build on it?

"We made changes as we went along," said Ron. "I had to be

fair to existing players and give them the chance to show what they could do, but there wasn't much time to mess about because we didn't want to spend half the season in experimenting!"

The season developed into one of ups and downs. There were some unexpected defeats but there were also some great victories — including a 5-2 away win at Tottenham and successes over Liverpool and Arsenal. When the final count was taken in May 1992, Villa finished in seventh place, ten positions higher than in the previous season. A trophy or two would have been nice but the improvement was satisfactory.

"We were fairly happy with that but we knew that we had to do better still the following season," said Ron Atkinson. "The whole point was to create a side capable of winning things. That was our objective and we did not stray from that."

The first three games of the 1992-93 season all had the same 1-1 scoreline. The fourth game was a 1-0 defeat at Everton. Villa's start in the new Premier League was less than good and there were a few groans from the terraces. Gradually, however, the act was got together and, when Villa faced Liverpool at home in the middle of September, the 37,863 crowd saw one of the best games at Villa Park for several years. The icing on the cake was a 4-2 win for Villa, with Dean Saunders scoring twice and Dalian Atkinson and Garry Parker adding one apiece. It was a turning point as the side suffered only two more defeats in their next sixteen games and rose to the top of the table.

Everyone was getting excited. That is, everyone except Ron Atkinson who earlier in the season had said, "Don't expect Villa to win the championship. I honestly don't think we will win it. We just aren't good enough yet. We need to sign more players if we are to take the title. We will finish higher than last season.

Last season's performance was not bad and we did finish in a reasonable position considering all the changes that we made. I've moved about twenty players in and out of the club since I came here and so we've had to make a lot of changes. That makes it much more difficult to get a regular pattern of play. Our target is a place in Europe and that means that we must finish in the top four. I'm not expecting anything better than that!"

Was that a bit of Atko kidology and did he really mean it?

"No, I meant it! As it turned out, I was right."

He was nearly wrong though. Villa surprised themselves by holding the top spot for several weeks and it looked as if they could well become the inaugural champions of the new Premier League. Ron Atkinson refused to budge in his opinion.

"We had a decent team but that was all — nothing to shout about. At times we did look a very good side and we did show a lot of character, but I maintained all along that we were not so special that we were the champions-elect. All we were doing was keeping ourselves in the leading pack. I had been there before and I knew what can happen in the closing weeks of a season. I would not kid myself that we were certainties for the title."

Ron Atkinson knew what he was talking about. Three defeats in the last three games of the season confirmed that the championship would not be going to Aston Villa. It went instead to Manchester United who won each of their last seven games and knocked Villa from the top spot. However, the depressing thoughts about what might have happened soon gave way to the realisation of what had actually happened. Villa had finished second in the table and were in Europe once again. There was something to celebrate after all.

"We were simply not the finished article," said Ron Atkinson as he scanned the transfer possibilities again. "We are getting there but we still need a few more options."

The quest for glory in the UEFA Cup was ended in the second round and the FA Cup ended in the fifth round — but the League Cup proved to be the highlight of the season — although it might well have become too much of a preoccupation as Premiership results fluctuated when the League Cup was at its most interesting. At one time Villa reached second place in the table but eventually had to make do with tenth position by the end of the season. It was made to look worse by a 2-1 home defeat by Arsenal and then two heavy defeats away — 5-1 at Newcastle and 4-1 at Southampton. On the last day of the season, Dwight Yorke scored twice in front of 45,347 Villa Park fans to beat Liverpool 2-1, so everyone went home happy, but the League position could have been better. Still, there was a trophy in the cabinet. Villa had won a great tussle at Wembley to beat Manchester United, bring home the League Cup and guarantee European football. Things were still looking up.

At the end of the previous season, Ron Atkinson had serenaded the Holte End with a rendering of *My Way*. A year on he was still doing it his way and the fans were still happy.

There were eyebrows raised when John Fashanu was signed from Wimbledon, but the supporters were now used to the comings and goings of players so their surprise did not last long. The first games of the Premiership were drawn but steadily the results began to improve. Big Ron signed an extension to his contract and Inter-Milan were knocked out of the UEFA Cup. Things were looking quite reasonable. Then came a run during which only one point was taken from nine games and the board decided that it was time for some blood-letting. The victim of their execution was, of course, the manager. The parting of the ways was not without some acrimony. Atkinson felt that better days were just around the corner and that Villa had had more than their fair share of ill-fortune. The chairman, Doug Ellis, had other thoughts.

"You make your own luck in football, as you do in life," he said.

Atkinson was shocked by the decision.

"To say that I was stunned is, I can assure you, an understatement. I knew the players better than anyone and I know that they were capable of putting together seven wins on the bounce and changing everything. I appreciate that we had a bad run of results, nobody was more aware of that than me, and I was slogging my guts out to try to put that right. I was very confident that we would turn the corner. Make no mistake, whoever takes over has a good enough team at Aston Villa for the right results to come."

Within a short time the shock of Atkinson's departure was overshadowed by the furore surrounding the appointment of his replacement as Brian Little walked out on Leicester and returned to his old club to take up a new challenge.

"It created one almighty stink in Leicester. I had had a close relationship with the chairman up to that point and I can honestly say that I did nothing wrong. My agreement allowed for such an event and that was it. Martin George, the Leicester chairman, has since shaken my hand and I believe that things are good between us again. I hope so. I had been a player with Aston Villa for twelve years and I even worked in the commercial department for some time after that, so it was a bit like being invited to return home. I was apprehensive about following Ron. He is a hard act to follow and I thought that the change in management style might be hard too. He left me some classy players though, and a heck of a lot of good young-ters coming through."

A new manager meant another fresh start for the club even at that stage of the season. Ironically, Little's first game in charge was away to Leicester City.

"I was happy with the 1-1 draw and, to be truthful, I was even happier that the fixture was over and that I did not have to go back to Filbert Street again that season. It was an experience that I would not want to repeat too often!"

Things did change. In January, Brian Little was named "Manager of the Month" and Villa went eight games without defeat. As enthusiasm soared, Villa recorded their best win for 33 years when they beat Newcastle 7-1 — Tommy Johnson, a fairly recent signing, scoring a hat-trick. Just to prove that every silver lining does have a cloud though, Villa hit a bad streak again and found themselves battling for their Premiership lives before the end of the season. A draw at Norwich on the very last day sealed their safety — but it had been a bit too close for comfort. For Brian Little there was time to reflect on the season.

"I think that at one stage I was being too kind to everyone and we slipped. I learned a lesson from that and I think the players learned lessons too. It hadn't been a good season but, as we were still a Premiership side at the end of it, I think we were forgiven for that. The supporters could not go on being expected to forgive though, and so I knew that the next season had to count. I was looking for a place in the top six at least. I would not take the players on a pre-season tour in the summer of 1995 because I wanted us to have a very tough training period at Bodymoor. It was an important time for the coaching staff and myself to make our mark on the team."

Little was as good as his word and when the new season

kicked-off there were a lot of happy Villa fans after they saw their side beat Manchester United 3-1. The campaign progressed with more successes than failures. The nearest thing to a Premiership derby match was against Coventry, and on both occasions Villa won — 3-0 away and 4-1 at home, Savo Milosevic scoring five of those goals. Liverpool proved to be the thorn in the side. Not only did they inflict two Premiership defeats but they also repeated the performance in the FA Cup semi-final. On the bright side though, Villa were rarely out of the top five in the table and once again progressed in the League Cup, eventually returning to Wembley to give Leeds a 3-0 thrashing in the Final and once again guaranteeing European football at Villa Park for the next season.

"It was not a bad season. We were challenging all the major competitions and won one of them. We were also favourably considered to be among the top three sides in the country, so that was satisfying. Before the season had started I had sat down with the directors and told them that I expected us to be in a top six position and seriously challenging for one of the cups. I don't think they believed me at the time but that's the way it turned out.

"The coaching team worked well. Allan Evans, John Gregory and myself did most of the organising but we did not have heavy discussions, either among ourselves or with the players. We preferred to talk with the players on a one-to-one basis rather than get into crowded debates. I think it helps to achieve a more settled squad like that."

As the 1996-97 season dawned, Brian Little was hoping to build on the improvements shown.

"We had built a platform for a championship-winning side. We had perhaps progressed that far rather more quickly than many might have expected, but the truth was we had a strong squad of young players with ambition. We were very close to what we were seeking."

A 5-0 thrashing of Wimbledon — again — was one of the highlights of life at Villa Park in the 1996-97 season. It might not sound much but Wimbledon had just gone 19 games without defeat. Again more than half the season was spent in a top five position, which kept the pot boiling nicely — although the UEFA Cup and the two domestic cups were soon committed to memory. However, there were a few worries behind the scenes as Sasa Curcic, Paul McGrath and Mark Bosnich were all involved in disagreements with the management.

Perhaps there was irony in Little's answer to a question at a press conference at the time. He was asked if he dreaded the prospect of a vote of confidence from chairman Doug Ellis.

"If I fail he has to do what is right for the football club, so I don't have any hang-ups about that."

During that season, John Gregory had left the club in October and had become manager of Wycombe Wanderers. He had enjoyed working alongside Brian Little but was ambitious enough to want to be a manager himself one day, and when that day dawned in October 1996 he left a gap in the Villa coaching team. It was, perhaps, to be a relevant move.

The 1997-98 season began in disastrous fashion. Villa failed to score in any of their first three games and, at the end of their fourth game, they were at the bottom of the table with not one point to their name. Things improved of course, but then came another slump in the New Year and, at the beginning of March, Brian Little resigned.

"I was naturally disappointed but when you go into management you know that things like this are inevitable. We seemed to have lost our way a bit although I was optimistic that our League form would improve. We were still in Europe so the season was still alive — but I felt that it was the right decision to make."

As Little left, his former coach, John Gregory, arrived. Star names were being touted by the newspapers while Gregory was fairly quietly appointed. He had been a player and a coach at Villa and knew the set-up and most of the players.

"It was a great honour to be asked and a very exciting challenge," he said. "I had not been away from Villa Park long enough for much to have changed so when I returned I felt at home straight away. It was particularly exciting because we were still in the UEFA Cup. There was work to be done in the Premiership because we were not doing ourselves justice — however, once we began to get a few results right the confidence came back and we had a good end to the season."

They certainly did, finishing very strongly by winning all but one of their last eight games and guaranteeing themselves another shot at the UEFA Cup. They only just went out of that competition in the 1997-98 season by losing to Atletico Madrid at the quarter-finals stage on the away goal rule.

"There is a great will to be successful here at Villa Park," said Gregory. "The supporters have been superb and now it is pay-back time. Another championship season is long overdue. My ambition is to have that Premiership trophy paraded through the streets of Aston."

Since the end of World War Two, Aston Villa have had a total of seventeen managers. Of those seventeen, only one has steered Villa to the championship. That is to say — so far!

CHAPTER SIX

THE FANS

PERHAPS you have to go to Old Trafford, Anfield, or St James's Park to really appreciate Aston Villa fans. Whenever Villa are playing away at any of those grounds, the sheer vocal strength and fervour of the Villa faithful is a credit to the club.

"It is fantastic to go out for your warm-up and see the claret-and-blue en masse in the ground," said Dwight Yorke. "It really gives you a lift, and when they start calling your name it is like bumping into a bunch of your best mates. They really know how to support the side and even when things go badly they don't give up on you if they know that you are doing your best."

At Villa Park, of course, the atmosphere is just amazing.

"It's a cliché, but the fans really are like having an extra man on the pitch," said former player and manager, Ron Atkinson, who knows a thing or two about big, noisy crowds from his years as manager of clubs like Atletico Madrid, Manchester United, Sheffield Wednesday and Midlands rivals Coventry and West Brom. "The Villa supporters are greatly under-rated in my opinion. When football people chat about grounds and atmosphere they always seem to overlook Villa, yet I have found the supporters to be right up there with the likes of Liverpool, Manchester United and the other big clubs.

"I'll tell you something, they never go quiet. If things are going well they'll back you all the way. If things are going badly because the team are not performing they'll give you some stick. That's because they know what they are watching and they expect better. You can't fool them or patronise them. They know the game too well for any kidology. They were brilliant to me when I was there and I like to think that we had a good relationship. I thought they were marvellous — and I still do."

Villa have attracted many new fans in recent years but there are also those who have followed the team for decades. One of them is Alan Randall, famed throughout the world for his re-creation of George Formby. Alan has been a Villa fan since World War Two.

"Coventry was my local team because I lived in Bedworth, but there was something about Aston Villa that always appealed to me. There was a bus company with a depot about a quarter-of-a-mile from where I lived and you could get a coach there which took you direct to the ground. I think about half of Bedworth used to go. As you got near to Villa Park it was as if there was an army on the march. All you could see was people, wearing Villa hats and scarves and carrying rattles, walking towards the ground. There used to be bike parks in the neighbouring gardens and peanut sellers on every corner.

"For me as a boy it was all part of the magic. I used to collect cigarette cards in those days and it was fantastic for me to see the footballers who were in my collection actually coming to life. My favourite player was George Cummings. He was captain and a great defender — my hero in fact! I remember going to see a wartime international at Villa Park between

England and Scotland. It was 1944 and I wanted to see the great Stanley Matthews in action because I had never seen him before. Just before the game it was announced that he would not be playing as he had been away with Stoke and they were stuck in fog somewhere. There were about 70,000 people in the ground at the time but they were all well-behaved. I was very disappointed. When I got back home I told my parents and then said, 'I know why he didn't turn up. He was scared of George Cummings!' George, of course, played at full-back for Scotland.

"I did eventually get to see Stanley Matthews several times and he was every bit as good as people said he was — but he never did like playing against George Cummings.

"My other favourites of those days included Eric Houghton, who was the best penalty-taker in the game, Frank Broome who was a brilliant winger, Harry Parkes, the great right-half and Alan Wakeman, who was a tremendous goalkeeper. Those were the players I mostly went to see. I never really bothered with Coventry because they were really down-market compared with Villa. At Villa Park I could see the stars.

"When I used to play in the street outside our house in Bedworth, one of the kids I played with was a niece of Len Latham, the Villa player who became assistant-secretary at the club. One day she came out wearing a pair of Villa socks. I couldn't believe my eyes. You just could not buy stuff like that in those days and I was beside myself with envy. To add insult to injury, she was a girl — and girls were simply not entitled to wear football socks when I was a kid. I was mortally stricken with jealousy and I tried to swap just about everything I owned, including my right arm, for those socks. She would not do the deal though and I was forced to live with my envy. I still spoke to her occasionally, I was even polite — but I never forgave her!

"When I was fourteen I landed myself in big trouble at school. England were playing Wales at Villa Park in 1948 and I went along to see it. I was quite good at school, but there was no way that I was going to sit there struggling with algebra while Frank Swift, Tommy Lawton and the rest were playing just down the road. I took the day off and I really got it in the neck the following morning. I think my teacher's anger was accentuated by the fact that he had wanted to go to Villa Park but hadn't the nerve to take the time off. Just for the record, England won 1-0, so it was well worth getting my ear warmed.

"Those were great days to watch football. If I, as a boy, arrived a bit late and could not get a place near the front, I would find myself picked up and passed down the terraces like a parcel until I did finally reach the front. There was great camaraderie among the supporters. You never saw a fight or general violence and the whole atmosphere was like that of one big family. You didn't get the hostility between rival fans that you get today. There was a good atmosphere. Everyone wanted their side to win of course — but they didn't go to war over it.

"It's all so very different now. I'm not saying that it's not as good, just that it is different. Villa have had their ups and downs in recent years but they still have one of the best grounds in the country and, I believe, one of the finest teams. I can still see George Cummings and his men on the pitch but how well they would do in today's style of football I wouldn't like to say. But then, players — no matter how great — are just passing ships. It is the club that really matters and even today when I am on one of my cruises, or touring in Australia, I never miss listening for the Villa results. Aston Villa is my club and I am proud of them."

Today the art of being a football supporter has become much more sophisticated. The internet has opened news and information possibilities that can keep even the most distant fans bang up to date with match and club details. John Penlington has been a Villa fan for as long as he can remember, and he is quite an expert on the internet scene.

"I must have been about six when I first attended a Villa game in the late 1950s and I have been hooked ever since. At school we used to talk Villa, but now I talk to Villa fans all over the world by means of the internet. We are known as the Internet Villans and it might sound as if we are a bunch of international 'anoraks', but we are not. We are simply all dyed-in-the-wool Villa fanatics who love nothing better than to chat about the club.

"Communicating as we do on the internet gives us all a sense of belonging. There are more than 500 of us now and it's just like chatting in a pub. If there are a group of us communicating and someone makes some odd remark, the others will talk him or her down. Sometimes we communicate on a one-to-one basis, but very often there is a whole bunch of us. Steve Stride, the Villa club secretary, is very keen. We have a social life too.

"Before home matches we always meet at the Faculty & Firkin pub near Aston University. All the Internet Villans are aware of it and quite often fans who are visiting from overseas drop in and put a face to their names. I have made many new friends through the Internet Villans. We have members all over the world including the USA, Canada, Peru, Tokyo, Singapore and Scandinavia. For instance, we have a contact in Tokyo and in Kobe.

"Norm Crandles is a great example. He used to be a pop singer in the early sixties, then in 1966 he emigrated to Canada.

He has remained totally loyal to Aston Villa and even has AVFC1 as his car registration number. Norm told me that he once saw an advert in the *Toronto Herald* which simply said: 'I don't suppose there are any Aston Villa fans around here, are there?' He responded to the advert and met Geoff Green. Now there is a very healthy Canadian Aston Villa Supporters Club. We communicated through the internet and, in July 1997, my wife and I finally met up with them in Canada and we had a great time. Geoff Green is now in his eighties but he is a very active Villa fan and has team strips going back to the 1950s.

"When my wife and I went to Australia, we were met in Sydney by two blokes in Villa shirts who showed us around. We then flew to Brisbane and, once again, there was someone in a Villa shirt to meet us. He had booked our hotel and helped make our visit a really great one. Once again the internet drums had announced our movements.

"The Internet Villans also sponsor some of the players' kit. and we have an annual Christmas 'do'. We are, first and foremost, Villa nuts and, secondly, fans of the internet. In a sense I suppose we are the supporters of the 21st century."

Brian Evans is one of Villa's best-known supporters, certainly in the Midlands. He has barely missed a home match in more than 35 years of following the team.

"I was a little boy when I was first taken to Villa Park. We used to go on the bus which was always packed. I have taken a keen interest in everything to do with Aston Villa and I even got involved when there was a take-over because I was so desperate to see Villa get over its ailments and be put on the road to success where I felt that the club belonged."

Brian is a solicitor by profession and is a very serene man — except when Villa score! — and then the claret and blue destroys any hint of a pin-stripe as he leaps into the air with the rest of them.

Neil Rioch — brother of Bruce — himself a former Villa player and a youth international for England, is the man at the helm of the Aston Villa Former Players' Association. In that capacity he finds himself constantly in contact with the various groups of Villa fans.

"They are a great bunch, mad-keen on Villa and always looking for the positives of life. You meet all kinds of people — directors and executives, housewives, schoolkids, butchers, bakers and candle-stick makers. The thing that most strikes me is that they are always happy. Even if the club is going through a bad time you never hear them having a serious moan. They are always looking forward to the next game — always keeping up that strong belief that they have in the club. That is probably why, even at the worst times, Villa's crowds have always been the envy of many other clubs. When Villa were in the Third Division for a short time, all the other clubs were delighted because they were getting bumper crowds for their games against Villa. There is a very solid rock of support for this club that stays loyal throughout.

"The supporters don't just turn up on a match day either — I'm absolutely amazed by their energy. They all have their own busy lives to run and yet they still find time to organise and attend a huge number of social events. I know because I am contacted all the time and asked to arrange for former players to attend their meetings and functions. It is very much like being involved with a huge happy family!"

Mentioning Neil Rioch, who joined Villa from Luton with Bruce in 1969, there is a little known fact about him that trivia fans will love. When England played West Germany in the Final

VILLA IN THE BLOOD

of the 1966 World Cup, the ball went out of play within moments of the kick-off. Guess the name of the ball-boy who retrieved that ball. Yes, it was the very same Neil Rioch!

It seems that wherever you go in the world you will always find Villa fans. John Penlington has already told us of his travels and meetings with claret and blue stalwarts. There are branches of the Supporters' Club all over the world. The Australian branch, for instance, is very busy and is based in New South Wales in a place called Dee Why. The AVSC in England is always happy to help people meet them and other Villa fans around the world so, if you are organising a holiday or business trip, get in touch with them and they will be pleased to point you in the right direction. Whether you are heading for the Continent, Hong Kong, the USA, Canada, Australia or South Africa, you will find yourself among friends who are also Villa followers.

Not everybody goes to the length that Norman Crandles does. He not only has a car registration number AVFC 1, but he also has signs at each end of his swimming pool which read 'Holte End' and 'Witton End'. Nevertheless, everyone pours all their energy into one single cause — and that cause is Aston Villa! There are many unsung heroes who have rarely missed a game throughout the years and will cheerfully freeze in mid-winter, or roast in the summery beginning and end of each season. Why do they do it? John Penlington has the answer.

"They are a unique bunch of people. They are eternal optimists. They are dedicated to the club and it does not matter how bad the last result was, the next one is bound to be better. They are not the sort of people who follow one club after another, depending upon who is being successful at the time. This army of Villa fans is only interested in one club. They are faithful to the claret and blue. There is no other club for them — only opponents!"

The players too have always appreciated the great support they get from the fans, none more so than Gareth Southgate.

"We think the world of them. I can honestly say that if the result of a game goes against us, we feel terrible for the supporters. They never give up and give every game their best shot. When we are playing away they are there in large numbers and really let us know that they are with us. They know their stuff as well. I can remember a couple of seasons ago we were playing at Old Trafford and the United fans started singing, 'You've never done the double.' The Villa fans responded immediately with, 'Yes we have, yes we have, yes we have!' They knew that the club had indeed done the double at the end of the last century, and they made sure that those United fans were left in no doubt about it."

It was all very good-natured, but there was a lesson to be learned by anyone who believes that football fans — and Aston Villa fans in particular — don't know what they are talking about. They had better think again!

"When you are playing away in European games and see a band of your own supporters there, it always gives you a great lift. They are always very noisy and often shout louder and longer than the home team's fans. When we go out to play we want to win for them as much as for ourselves because we feel that we are representing them and we try to achieve on their behalf. They are like our team-mates and they deserve the best, which is why we get annoyed with ourselves if we feel that we haven't given our best. They never let us down and we do not like letting them down."

Goalkeepers probably appreciate the support more than

anyone because they spend so much more time closer to the fans, as Mark Bosnich explained.

"The Villa supporters are brilliant. Knowing they are behind you gives you a real lift, especially when you come out for the second half of an away match and you are defending the goal at the end where they are stationed. They always give you a fantastic welcome and it can really boost your confidence knowing that you have an army of mates right behind you. Some of their comments are hilarious, but they always know when to let you concentrate. They are a great bunch — the best."

The most amazing thing is that there is nobody at the club who is not a fan. Chairman Doug Ellis, the men on the turnstiles, the ground staff, car park attendants — absolutely everyone. They are all the same. They will laugh and cry with the club to a person. At quite a few clubs you will hear some members of staff claim that they never watch a game because they are not that interested. That is not the case at Villa. As Neil Rioch said, "I doubt that anyone could work at Villa without being a fan. It is such a family club — even though it is such a big club — that if you were not a fan you would probably feel like an intruder."

Today's highest profile fan is, of course, Nigel Kennedy, megastar violinist and claret and blue through and through. He goes to great lengths to get to Villa matches whenever possible and often turns up at European games both at home and away. He laments the passing of standing on the terraces and still prefers to be at the Holte End, helping to create the noise that Villa players consider to be like having an extra man in the team.

"I have followed Villa since I was little and my love for the club has just grown and grown," said Nigel. "I even arrange concert dates around match fixtures and I'll travel just about anywhere to see a game. I have had a car sprayed in Villa colours and I was one of the organisers of a petition to keep the terraces at Villa Park when all the clubs were ordered to change over to all-seater stadiums. I couldn't imagine Villa Park with no standing areas.

"I like the place now, I think it is a fantastic stadium, but I wish there was still an area for standing. I'm a very basic fan. I believe that football is a simple game meant to be played and watched for fun. That doesn't mean that it shouldn't be professional but it doesn't need to be too sophisticated. I like nothing better than to put on a Villa shirt and watch with the crowd from within the crowd. I shout and yell with the best of them.

"I have been in the directors' box quite a few times and they are a good bunch in there, although I think that some of them find me a little difficult because I do not act or dress in the way that they do. I have given them a recital once or twice, both at home and away matches, so we are all mates — I hope!

"I have been through good times and desperate times with Villa. I remember the championship season and the European Cup win as well as the successes at Wembley in the League Cup, and I have also been through relegation. I have cheered my head off and I have shed tears. I am sure that there are good times ahead. I can't wait to see the Premiership trophy paraded at Villa Park.

"Villa have had many great players during the time that I have been a supporter but I think that the current squad at the end of the 1990s is as good as any. There might be a few individuals from the past that I would like to see in a Villa shirt again — Andy Gray for one — but in over-all strength, I'm sure that we are close to becoming the team of the next decade.

"I shall still be there at Villa Park, and anywhere else they are playing, to cheer them on. What would life be without Aston Villa?"

That seems to be the philosophy of so many of the club's supporters. Let's have a final quote on the subject from someone who has never been at a loss for words. Tommy Docherty really summed up the relationship between Aston Villa and its supporters when he said, "If you hung out 11 shirts at Villa Park on a Sunday morning, 10,000 supporters would turn up to watch them dry."

CHAPTER SEVEN

GOALKEEPERS

GOALKEEPERS are a breed on their own! They even wear different clothes from the rest of the team. Some say they are all one sandwich short of a picnic, while others say that they are intellectually superior because they do not run around as much as the rest. For decades, before and after the war, the goalkeeper's trademark was a green roll-neck sweater and a flat cap. Then in the 1970s there came a kind of goalie revolution with new lines in sweaters, headgear and thick gloves.

What was it like to be a goalkeeper for Aston Villa in the early 1970s? Jim Cumbes led a high-profile life during that time because he did not restrict his activities to football. Jim was also a pretty good cricketer, a fast bowler for Worcestershire, and he still represents Lancashire at veterans level when time allows. He is kept very busy as chief executive of Lancashire County Cricket Club. Football, cricket and administrative skills were not Jim's only talents.

He joined Villa in November 1971 having already made his mark at Tranmere Rovers and West Bromwich Albion. He signed for Villa with a good reputation and certainly did not disappoint anyone.

"My first game was against Oldham. Villa were in the Third Division at the time and working hard to get out of it. We won my debut game 6-0. I remember Andy Lochhead getting a hat-trick. The next game was a 3-0 win over Bradford, and then we beat Bolton 3-2 so it was all going very well. We clinched promotion with three games still to go and we were champions with one game left.

"On the last game of the season we were presented with the trophy and beat Bournemouth 1-0. There was a great atmosphere in Villa Park with nearly 50,000 fans celebrating. Mind you, one of my proudest moments was a couple of months earlier when we played Santos in a friendly at Villa Park and beat them 2-1. It was a great occasion and I think 55,000 turned up to see us. Well, a few probably came to see Pele I suppose!"

What Jim Cumbes modestly forgets to mention is that Villa lost only three Division Three games after he joined, and he kept 18 clean sheets in 29 matches

"Jim gave the defence a lot of confidence," said Chris Nicholl, who had joined as a centre-half from Luton in that same season. "He was boss of the area as all good goalkeepers should be. He had tremendous agility and pulled off many a save that seemed impossible. He had a good positional sense too and, contrary to the popular image of goalkeepers, he had a good brain."

As we've already said, there was much more to Jim Cumbes than football and cricket. In those days he was a bachelor living in Edgbaston and he certainly knew his way around the kitchen.

"I have always enjoyed a big breakfast, so I made sure that I had a really good one every morning. Then I would cook a decent meal, sometimes for the other lads too, in the evening.

Fish and chips were all right now and then — but not too often!"

After training in the morning he would get down to business in the afternoon.

"I was very aware that a sportsman's life is a short one and so I wanted to invest something in my future. When Bert Williams, the former Wolves and England goalkeeper, decided to sell his sports goods business, John Osborne, my fellow goalkeeper at West Bromwich, and I went into partnership to buy it. We did well and it gave us something to do in the afternoons."

With mornings and afternoons taken care of — and, of course, one or two games each week — Jim Cumbes could not have been blamed for having a rest on Sunday mornings …but no! On Sunday mornings Jim used to host his own show on BBC Radio Birmingham.

"It was a hectic life but that's how I enjoyed it. I don't blame any player, then or now, for wanting to take it easy, but I just couldn't. If I had ever felt that my outside activities were interfering with my football I would have given them up. Football always came first."

After Jim Cumbes came John Burridge, one of the craziest 'keepers of all time. Yes it is true that, when he married, he took his weights with him on honeymoon so that he could keep fit! And yes, he has been known to wear his gloves, and even his boots, in bed — just to 'wear them in'. However, beneath that eccentric exterior there is a very talented goalkeeper who has been on the scene for nearly thirty years. He has changed clubs more than two dozen times and one of those changes took him to Aston Villa in September 1975, the club paying £100,000 to sign him from Blackpool.

"He was a very good goalkeeper," said Chris Nicholl. "He didn't stay with us that long but during his couple of years he helped the club to reach fourth place in the League and win the League Cup in 1977. He organised his defence well and he gave them confidence because he was not only very solid but he was also very agile. His positioning was excellent and he really worked hard at his fitness. You could say that he was a fanatic about fitness. When Jimmy Rimmer came to the club John Burridge became second choice and I don't think he wanted to stay like that. Anyway, after a loan spell with Southend he was bought by Crystal Palace. He has travelled a fair bit since and I think he enjoys being on the move quite often."

Burridge vividly recalls his Villa days.

"I had a good time at Aston Villa. We were in the First Division and we improved our position in the League while I was there. We also had that League Cup marathon Final against Everton in which I was honoured to play and collect a winner's medal. It was a happy club as well. Everyone seemed to get on with each other. I certainly have happy memories of being at Villa Park."

Jimmy Rimmer also has happy memories of his Villa days.

"I had started my career at Manchester United but it was not working out. I was always close to first-team football, but Alex Stepney was always in good form and hardly ever injured and so my chances were very limited. Harry Gregg gave me the chance to go to Swansea on loan. He was the manager and joining him was the best thing I ever did. He completely transformed me and, to tell the truth, I owe it to him that I had a first-class career. He spent a lot of time with me during my loan spell and, when I returned to Old Trafford in early 1974, Arsenal became interested in me and signed me. Then, in the summer of 1977, Villa signed me and I became first-choice goalkeeper for the next six years. I think you could count the number of games that I missed on your fingers.

"Ron Saunders was the manager and I found him to be a great boss. He was very hard, and tough on discipline, but he was always fair. If you played well you stayed in. If you didn't, he would give you the chance to put your performance right — but if you didn't then you were out. It was quite simple but at least you knew where you stood with him.

"I was at Aston Villa for six years until I left in the middle of the 1982-83 season. I missed only one League match in all that time. There was a very good squad at Villa in those days and we achieved the championship and success in Europe. I was always impressed by the size of the club. That might sound a bit strange coming from someone who had been with Manchester United and Arsenal, but somehow Villa has an amazing ability to be a huge club with the atmosphere of a small, close-knit family. I don't think we have seen the best of Villa yet. I believe they have some really good times to come in the future."

Nigel Spink's story of how he came to win a European Cup medal is covered in another part of this book, but we cannot ignore a goalkeeper who served Villa well for an amazing nineteen years. It is even more amazing when you consider that he was signed by the club almost by accident. An Essex lad, he looked set to enter the game with West Ham but, because the Hammers had Mervyn Day in sparkling form, they decided not to offer professional terms to Nigel Spink. Instead he joined his home-town club of Chelmsford City.

"I thought I was destined for life in non-League football. Jimmy Greaves was playing for them at the time and I thought that he was as near as I was likely to get to the big-time."

Jimmy Greaves remembers him well.

"I was playing in midfield for Chelmsford but I don't think I ever made a tackle so, because of me, young Nigel certainly had plenty of practice. I remember when he was signed by Aston Villa at the start of 1977 he had a bit of luck on his side. Chelmsford had another really good young goalie called Nicky Penn. It was him who Villa wanted to sign. Nicky didn't want a career as a professional, so Villa took Nigel instead!"

Nigel Spink agrees with that version of events and also recalls that even when he joined Villa he did not become an overnight success.

"I was in the Reserves for ages. Jimmy Rimmer was always first choice. I did get a first-team game on Boxing Day 1980, and we lost 2-1 to Nottingham Forest so it wasn't a debut to remember. I never played in the first team again until that night of the European Cup Final. Throughout the time Jimmy Rimmer was very encouraging and reminded me that he had been in the same position at Old Trafford. He said that I would get my chance one day. He was right of course, and later when he had left I became first choice."

The £4,000 Villa handed to Chelmsford when they signed him proved to be a great investment as Nigel became the club's longest-serving player with 460 first-team appearances to his credit.

"I regret not being in a championship side while I was with the club, but I have an England cap, a League Cup medal, and the European medals as souvenirs so, all in all, it was a good move for me. I grew to love the club and it was a big wrench when I left. Aston Villa gets in your blood."

For a time Les Sealey replaced Nigel Spink. The Villa fans soon saw why he had the same reputation as John Burridge for being a little eccentric, but nevertheless a good and heroic goalkeeper. Nigel Spink returned to first-team action and Sealey moved on.

Villa have had many fine goalkeepers over the years. Joe Rutherford joined the club just before World War Two and was still there after it finished to provide a safe pair of hands, along with Alan Wakeman, as Villa moved into the 1950s. Keith Jones was also there, a Welsh international whom Villa found playing for Kidderminster Harriers. He kept the goal safe until early 1956 when the incomparable Nigel Sims arrived.

Sims was a big man standing over six feet and weighing more than 14 stones. Yet he had the agility and athleticism of a winger.

"He was a tremendous goalkeeper, very under-rated in my opinion," said Alan Deakin, who played in front of many great goalkeepers.

Geoff Sidebottom and Colin Withers were two more of the great Villa goalkeepers of the past, and there is no doubt that the club has always had a fine array of custodians.

Older supporters might say that they don't make 'em like that any more — and yet the younger generation will say, "What about Mark Bosnich?" Yes indeed, what about Mark Bosnich?

Bosnich is at the very least a character, and at the most a sensational goalkeeper. When Manchester United failed to get a work permit for Bosnich in 1989, it seemed that his career in British football had been and gone.

"I had a dream start at Old Trafford, playing three first-team games and getting rave reviews. It all turned sour when they could not get me a work permit. To be fair they tried everything, but after a while I resigned myself to the fact that I was not going to stay at United, or even play in England. I went for a trial at

Brondby but I couldn't settle, so I went home to Australia to play for Sydney Croatia. Even that went wrong as I was sent off in my fourth game and dropped. I thought my career was really over then. That is, until Villa came for me which took everyone by surprise."

Bosnich married a girl from Manchester and signed for Villa at near enough the same time. His work permit problem was at an end and his career was able to start properly.

"I know for a fact that Alex Ferguson was upset. People thought that I had played a dirty trick on him, even members of my own family. However, I had to think of my future and joining Villa was an opportunity that I could not afford to miss. At first I was understudy to Nigel Spink but then I was given my first-team chance."

Bosnich has since earned a reputation as a penalty saver, been embroiled in a row with Tottenham fans, and of course picked up a collection of caps as an Australian international and a couple of League Cup winner's medals. He has also had the indignity of having a penalty put past him by a rabbit. He is something of a fitness fanatic and his warm-up routine is something he continues to do DURING each game. It was Ron Atkinson who signed him for Villa.

"I knew he had a lot of potential. I had seen him at Old Trafford as a trainee. He was always very keen, very ambitious, willing to listen and work hard, and he just had that special something about him that told you he would be a very capable goalkeeper."

Bosnich was delighted, of course, when he arrived back in this country to restart his career.

"You can imagine how I felt when I arrived at Villa Park. All those reserve games and training that I had done at Old

Trafford had some meaning at last. I had been starting to think that it had all been for nothing. I was thrilled to join Villa, another big club with ambitions to match my own. Much has happened since then and they have made me quite a celebrity in Australia where I am looked upon as some sort of role model. I try my best to encourage young Australian players to work hard to fulfil their own ambitions."

The role model bit might have become slightly tarnished after that bizarre and unseemly incident at White Hart Lane, when Bosnich responded to taunts from Tottenham fans by giving them a Nazi salute which many interpreted as being a racist response to a club well known for its Jewish following. The incident was splashed about the media as if it were the outbreak of World War Three, but it was put into perspective by Bosnich himself who was fined £1,000 by the Football Association.

"It was a stupid thing for me to do, but I meant no serious harm and the whole thing was blown out of all proportion. I am a young boy who made a mistake and that's the way it goes. I do not normally have a big problem with fans and I have an especially great relationship with the Villa fans. I have often heard rumours about me leaving the club, but I like it at Villa and I love the city of Birmingham. I am in no hurry to leave just yet."

The incident was indeed blown out of all proportion. MPs even found ways of having their voices heard, although none of those who were passing judgement were at the match. Ugo Ehiogu was at the game though, and saw the whole thing.

"We watched a lot of *Fawlty Towers* on the team coach to and from games, and I can understand how Mark might have reacted by copying Basil Fawlty in one of the episodes. Having said that, I don't think he even did it with the right arm, so there was nothing remotely serious about it. It is to Mark's credit that he didn't hide. He went to London to speak to Alan Sugar, the Tottenham chairman, and even offered to meet the Spurs' fans at a forum. That takes some guts but Mark wanted to get it out of the way so that he could get on with his football."

Brian Little was manager at the time and he also saw the incident.

"Bossy is a very nice guy who would never intentionally offend people. He was trying to have a bit of repartee with the crowd. Unfortunately, he didn't make a very good job of it!"

The final word about that incident is that Bosnich is an Australian of direct Croatian descent, and has a close association with the divides of politics and racism. Not only that but one of his favourite aunts is Jewish!

Anyway, what about his name as a penalty saver? He once made five penalty saves in one week and that enhanced his reputation as a super-stopper. He himself, however, always plays down his apparent specialist ability.

"I don't really have a special way of saving penalties. You can work on it as much as you like but it all goes out of the window when you are actually in a game. I just try to hold myself for as long as possible — right up to the player's final step — before committing myself to action. I usually look at their non-kicking boot to see which way to go, but you can wait and wait and wait and they will still just stick it right in the corner. It's more luck than anything else. If you manage to save it you become a hero — if you don't, nobody blames you!"

Don't be fooled by that last statement. Every time a goal is conceded, Bosnich feels it like a stab wound.

"The whole point of being a goalkeeper is to stop the ball going into the net. If you don't then you have lost one. If you take it too personally you can ruin your confidence, but if you don't feel it at all you probably shouldn't be playing. I feel it for the supporters too. It's a big disappointment when the other side scores."

He has had his fair share of injuries too, including a broken ankle and knee problems. He has had several close encounters with the surgeons but he is still incredibly fit.

"You have to be fit to give of your very best. You are paid to be a professional footballer and therefore you should not shirk your responsibilities. One of those responsibilities is to the supporters too. They pay to see you at your peak and so you should be doing the best you can for them. The Villa fans are really excellent. I would love to win the championship for them because they truly deserve it."

Of course, having a penalty put past you by a rabbit might not be exactly confidence-boosting for your defenders!

"That was at a press do. This bloke from a cable television company was dressed up as a seven-foot rabbit. There were a lot of journalists and PR men there and I don't think I had let one penalty past me unless it was going well wide — which most of them did. Suddenly this 'rabbit' steps up and, as he let fly, his foot came off and flew through the air. As I went to grab it I noticed the ball going into the other side of the net and it was too late for me to stop it. You have to admit that it's a bit disconcerting to see a fluffy foot coming towards you!"

Aston Villa have a great tradition of excellent goalkeepers, but Mark Bosnich is truly unique in being fooled by a seven-foot rabbit whose foot certainly brought him no luck!

There is no doubt that in the years to come there will be many more Villa goalkeepers who hog the headlines for one reason or another — but let's face it, the Villa guys have been pretty good so far!

CHAPTER EIGHT

IN DEFENCE

IF YOU are playing for glory don't bother being a defender. Your job is to stop the opposition, to stay back in the trenches while the heroes are spraying the ball about at the other end of the battlefield. If the opposition attack, you kill it off with a minimum of fuss and bother. The better you carry out your job the less you will be noticed. It is as simple as that. However, even the unsung stars of defence deserve some acknowledgment. After all, Villa have had some great defenders in the past as indeed they have now.

In the immediate post-war period, full-backs were expected to be tough guys who were big on bone-crunching and short on finesse. But in George Cummings, Villa had a man who was as hard as nails but who also brought an extra quality to the art of defence in that he could delicately distribute the ball to set up an attack for his own side. A Scot, he joined Villa at the end of 1935 for £9,500 from Partick Thistle and stayed with the club until he retired in 1949.

In 1945 he took over as captain from Alex Massie and kept the job until his retirement — a tribute to his leadership skills and the fact that there was more to the man than big boots and flashing studs. As the late Eric Houghton once said:

"George Cummings was a typical Scottish defender. He tackled like an express train and few, if any, players bested him over ninety minutes. He was also a gentleman with a good brain, a quiet sense of humour and a very distinct love of football. He was always a good man to have around, whether you were in the middle of a game or just sitting in a cafe having a cup of tea. I never ever saw him panic. He was always in control. He used to be called 'icicle' because he was always so cool."

With George Cummings at No 3, Villa had few worries on their left side of defence, while on their right side they had one of the fastest defenders ever to wear the No 2 shirt in Vic Potts — a local lad who began his career with Tottenham who later released him before he was able to stake his claim for a first-team place. Their loss was Villa's gain, but not immediately because Doncaster signed him first. When war broke out he returned to Aston and played as a guest for Villa. Needless to say, the club then signed him on properly and he had a number of happy years at Villa Park before injury forced him to hang up his boots in 1949 and venture into scouting and coaching.

"He was very fast indeed," recalls Harry Parkes. "He could easily have been a winger but he preferred to be in defence. Many's the time I have seen an opposition player get the ball and think he could easily outpace Vic Potts. Before he knew what had happened he would be on the ground and Vic would be sprinting away with the ball. He was an excellent full-back and would easily have fitted into today's style of play.

"We had a very good defence in those days with Cummings and Potts at the back and Frank Moss at centre-half. He was a very tough player too, but he was also extremely skilful. He was excellent with his head and was an expert at man-marking."

That testimony was borne out by the late great Tommy Lawton, who believed that Frank Moss was the toughest opposing centre-half he ever had to face.

"I never got a kick when Frank was marking me. He was a great player — hard, but fair," said Lawton.

Moss had joined Villa in 1938 and stayed until 1955. His brother Amos also wore the claret and blue, as did their father — also called Frank, who captained both Villa and England between the World Wars. The Moss family were quite a dynasty for Aston Villa.

It is no wonder that in the immediate post-war years, with Cummings, Potts and Frank Moss providing the last line of defence before the goalkeeper, Villa had such a reputation for being one of the most difficult sides to score against.

As the 1950s dawned, Harry Parkes began to wear the No 2 shirt quite often and was regularly partnered by Dickie Dorsett on the left side. Dorsett was something else — a tough man in every sense of the word. There are legends of how he would burst through the pain barrier in order to play. It is said that once he even had a septic tooth pulled without the benefit of anaesthetic so that he would not miss a match. He even grew a beard for a while which made him look even more wild and woolly.

"Dick was one of the hardest men I have ever known," said Harry Parkes. "He was tremendous in the tackle and never flinched, even if he got the ball smacked into his face. I have seen him play through injuries which would have floored other players. He was quite a character."

Peter Aldis was the last Villa left-back to win the FA Cup.

Earlier he had played at centre-forward, but Villa transformed him and he established himself in the No 3 shirt for 300 first-team appearances — not bad for a guy who looked destined to spend his life making chocolate in the Cadbury's factory.

Peter McParland was in that same Cup Final team.

"Peter was a lovely man and a very good footballer. He was always cheerful and seemed to have a constant smile, even when things were going against us. He skippered the side for a season and proved himself to be a good leader. He was a very competent defender who worked hard and never gave the opposition an inch. yet he was always very good-natured. I remember he had overcome some injury problems to re-establish himself in the side and he always commanded the respect of his team-mates."

Another of the club's favourite defenders was Jimmy Dugdale. He was also in the side which won the FA Cup in 1957, but there was more to his game than just that one success as Johnny Dixon remembers.

"Jimmy was Mr Reliable. He played his heart out at centre-half in every game. Not much got past him in the air and he was also a good tackler. He was a past master at killing an opposition attack and immediately setting us up with a well-placed pass or header."

As well as picking up the FA Cup medal, Jimmy Dugdale was also in the Villa side that won the League Cup in 1961, a fitting tribute to his contribution to the game.

It is impossible to mention great defenders of that era without including Stan Lynn.

"Stan was a great player," said Johnny Dixon. "He could tackle, he could beat opponents with sheer ball skill, and he was one of the best dead-ball kickers I have ever seen. He could do all the sorts of tricks from a free-kick that you see the Brazilians doing now, and he had such power as well. Marvellous player."

In the 1960s Charlie Aitken was probably the star defender. He began his Villa career in 1961 and remained at the club until 1976, making more than 660 first-team appearances. To describe him as one of the all-time greats would be almost an understatement as he made the No 3 shirt his own for a record 561 League appearances.

"He was a marvellous servant for Aston Villa," remembers Alan Deakin. "He rarely had a bad game in all that time and but for him the bad times could have been much worse. The supporters thought the world of him and he is still looked upon as a legend. He had all the attributes of a quality full-back. He was tough when he needed to be , but always constructive. He was the sort of player who inspired everyone around him. If you started feeling a bit tired you only had to look at Charlie and you would get your second wind. I'm amazed that he never won a senior Scotland cap. They don't know what they missed!"

Mick Wright and Keith Bradley were two outstanding right-backs for Villa in the 1960s and 70s, and both chalked up an impressive list of appearances. Mick Wright played more than 315 games in the claret and blue, while Keith Bradley played 143 first-team matches. Following them came two other great Villa characters, Chris Nicholl and John Gidman.

It's funny to think that Chris Nicholl, who was at one time the most expensive player ever to be signed by a Third Division club, was only valued at £500 during his early career.

"I began with Burnley, but they didn't think that I would make the grade and so they released me. I went into non-League football with Witton Albion until Alan Ball Senior spotted me. He was manager of Halifax at the time and did a deal with them to sign me for £500. That really kick-started my career and, if it had not been for that move, I doubt that I would ultimately have had the pleasure of playing for Aston Villa."

After 42 games for Halifax, Nicholl joined Luton for £75,000. They were then in the First Division so it came as a shock when he agreed to join Villa early in 1972. Few players like to move down a division until later in their careers.

"It didn't bother me. I had seen a much worse dive in my career when I left Burnley so dropping down a division didn't worry me at all. I was certain that the drop down was only a temporary measure. Of course, we won promotion soon afterwards so my belief in the club's future was not only justified but thoroughly vindicated."

Nobody was more delighted to see Villa promoted than Luton. They then made a profit on the transfer. Villa paid £75,000 to sign Nicholl but also agreed to pay an extra £15,000 if he was in the first-team squad when the club gained promotion. He was and they did!

"We all knew that the club was on the move. We were pulling in big crowds and everything at Villa was geared to the top division. It became a burning ambition of mine to wear the claret and blue in the First Division, and I'm pleased to say that I made it. It was at the end of the 1974-75 season that we knew we were promoted as runners-up to Manchester United. We had scored more goals than anyone else in the top two divisions and our defence record was bettered only by Manchester United in the entire Football League.

"Our defence was well-organised and very confident. When you have players like Dennis Mortimer, John Robson and John Gidman around you, to name just a few, you cannot help but play well.

"I had a terrific few years at Villa. We re-established the club as a major force in English football and twice won the League Cup while I was with the club. I even had the honour of captaining the side in 1977 so I can honestly say that the best days of my playing career were when I was with Aston Villa."

Talking about John Gidman, his career was given a new lease of life when he joined Villa in 1972.

"I had started at Liverpool but they gave me a free transfer which is quite a blow when you are a young lad with dreams. It's a bit like being offered something you really like and then being denied it. It is better not to have been offered it in the first place. It was a sickening blow to my pride.

"When Villa gave me a chance I was all the more determined to prove myself. I had been a bit depressed but I found a new appetite for the game in the Midlands. Having been playing as a midfielder, it was not easy to adjust to being a defender and I sometimes got a bit of stick for going upfield too much. However, I always recovered quickly, and if I had anything at all it was speed. It was often said that I was the fastest full-back in the Football League, but that was not something which could be proved one way or the other."

John Gidman had eight happy years at Villa before moving on. Today he has a business in Spain, but he still follows Villa's fortunes.

"I get the results as quick as I can and I still keep in touch with some of the other former players who let me know what is going on. My hair isn't as long as it used to be during my Villa days but I still get recognised.

"It was a privilege to be part of the set-up that took the club back to the First Division. Brian Little was also around at the time and I think his hair was even longer than mine. He was one of a bunch of great Villa players who had knitted into a strong side.

"Probably one of my greatest memories was beating Liverpool 2-1 at Anfield in November 1977. Andy Gray scored both goals and was very sportingly given an ovation by the Kop. It wasn't just that we beat Liverpool — I wasn't bitter or anything like that — it was that we had ended their record of going 20 months without a home defeat. When I left Villa in 1980 I joined Everton, so my games against Liverpool continued to hold an extra meaning.

"I had a good career as a player but it might never have happened if Villa had not given me that chance. I still appreciate that and I hope that as a player I repaid that debt in some small way."

It has often been said that defenders are accident prone. John Gidman, Villa and England right-back, was surely a case in point. He suffered two injuries which were not only career-threatening but life-threatening as well!

The worst incident was in November 1974 when he was established in the No 2 shirt for Villa, having progressed through the youth team after being rejected by Bill Shankly at Liverpool.

"I was at a Guy Fawkes Night bonfire party when a firework exploded in my face. It was horrendous. I couldn't see a thing for some time and I was quite badly burned. It was touch and go as to what condition I would be in, but the hospital staff were brilliant and sorted me out. Even so, I did not play again for nearly six months and I thought that it was all over for me before I had really got started."

It was not his only close encounter with mortality either. When Villa were playing away to Norwich he had an accident in the dressing-room which also took him to the brink.

"I opened a window — it was as simple as that. The trouble was that it had been painted over and when I forced it the glass smashed and slashed open my wrist. The blood poured out and to save time the police took me to the hospital in one of their cars. Waiting for an ambulance might have taken just a little too long. The doctors told me that I was more lucky than I could imagine because not only was the cut just an inch away from a main artery but it was less than an inch from severing tendons. It shook me up a bit because I did bleed quite a lot and the realisation that I could have bled a lot more was a bit frightening to say the least.

"I suppose it could be said that I was a bit clumsy — but I know that I wasn't. In both cases it was one of those things that could have happened to anyone. It just happened to be me!"

When you start to think about great Villa defenders it is difficult to know where the list ends. It would be impossible to overlook Fred Turnbull, who played close to 200 competitive games for the club in the late 1960s and early 70s. Although a Geordie, Fred loved Aston Villa and was a keen servant of the club until his career was brought to a premature end by injury.

"I remember the moment as if it were yesterday," he said. "We were playing against Bristol City at Ashton Gate in March 1973. I was standing facing my own-goal when two City forwards lunged for the ball. One hit me above the knee and the other below. I knew then that it wasn't good and when I got home, my wife Joan, who is an experienced physiotherapist, took one look and said that I had damaged my cruciate ligament — a diagnosis which was confirmed very shortly afterwards. Then came the months and months of fighting for a lost cause."

A year later Turnbull returned, but it was only a very

temporary come-back. After a couple of games he was forced into retirement.

"It was a dreadful feeling, knowing that you were finished. Villa granted me a testimonial, which I really appreciated, and then it was all over. I missed the day-to-day involvement and all the banter in the dressing-room and, of course, that special atmosphere on a match day. You never know what you have got until you haven't got it any longer!"

The names come thick and fast. Colin Gibson defended for Villa for eight seasons, purely because Portsmouth made the mistake of not offering him terms after having him on their books as an associate schoolboy. What a move it turned out to be for Gibson who won a championship medal and a European Super Cup medal. In 1985 he was transferred to Manchester United but still has fond memories of his Aston Villa days.

"I had a great time at Villa. I was introduced to the first team by Ron Saunders, who was a very strict manager, and I think he was very good for me. You could not give him second-best and get away with it. I was also privileged to be part of a successful squad during one of the best periods in Villa's recent history."

Colin Gibson almost shared the No 3 shirt with Gary Williams who was often selected as a defender although he could, and did, play just about everywhere except in goal. Gary Williams has the unusual distinction of helping another team win promotion while he was a Villa player.

"I went out on loan to Walsall as I was recovering from an injury and I was there when they won promotion from the Fourth Division. The following season I won a League championship medal with Villa and the season after that I collected a European Cup medal. It was a good run for me."

Also involved with the championship season of 1980-81 was Ken McNaught, a tough Scottish centre-half and the son of a Scottish international.

"He was a rugged sort of a player who knew no fear, exactly what you want in the centre of your defence," said Peter Withe, who was a team-mate for three years.

Kenny Swain, Tony Dorigo, Bernard Gallacher, Kevin Gage, Chris Price, Stuart Gray, and the mighty Paul Elliott all made their individual marks in the Villa defence, as did Derek Mountfield who enjoyed three happy seasons with Villa before being signed by Wolves in 1991.

Allan Evans could never have known that he was going to have such a long association with Aston Villa when he journeyed south from Dunfermline at the request of Ron Saunders in 1977. Evans was a part-timer with Dunfermline while working as a store manager, although he was also a qualified insurance broker. Ron Saunders had invited him for a trial.

"I remember that after just three days I was so shattered that I could hardly stand. Fortunately Villa decided that I had done enough to clinch my transfer and that was that."

Villa paid £30,000 and in so doing bought a defender who was destined to play a major role in their League championship and European Cup successes. But it was tough going for Evans at the start.

"I was a little bit raw and naive, so I had a few disciplinary problems in my first few years with Villa. I gradually learned though and came to terms with the situation. We had a good squad throughout my playing years with Villa. We had several managers too. I owe a lot to different managers at Villa but I would have to put Graham Taylor at the very top of the pile. His arrival was like a breath of fresh air. He said the club was a shambles and he was spot on. We needed a good shake-up and he provided it."

Allan Evans remained at Villa Park until 1990 when he was released and went to Australia. Later on, though, he returned to Aston Villa as assistant to Brian Little, still putting to good use all that he had learned as a player at the club — and indeed during his teen years at Dunfermline. Anyone who makes their senior debut as a 16-year-old playing for Dunfermline against Rangers and breaks their leg on that debut must be worth paying attention to.

In the last few seasons, several names have been prominent in defence. Steve Staunton, Ugo Ehiogu, Paul McGrath, Alan Wright, and Gary Charles, to name but a few. Gareth Southgate has been one of the most prominent, but we shall be talking to Gareth rather more in our chapter on captains. Instead, let us consider a player who is probably one of the most under-rated defenders in Europe.

Dwight Yorke often plays against Steve Staunton in training and has first-hand knowledge of him as both team-mate and opponent.

"He has a great left foot whether he is tackling, passing or shooting. His role as a defender allows him to get into attack quite a lot and you often find him popping up in scoring positions. He's a quiet lad who takes everything in his stride, but he is also a top-class player."

Steve Staunton joined Villa in August 1991 for £1.1 million after five years with Liverpool. He was already an international with the Republic of Ireland but the move certainly enhanced his career.

"Joining Villa was a great move for me. I was not unhappy

with Liverpool, but I felt that joining Villa would provide me with a much greater challenge and the chance to improve my game. It was a good decision because I have been given much greater freedom to play things my own way. I have always enjoyed getting forward without neglecting my job as a defender and at Villa I have been able to do that. Not only that but Villa is a tremendous club to be playing for. The facilities are great and the atmosphere is terrific. There is always a family feel about the club and I like that. It has widened my playing horizons too because I have sometimes played as a central defender as well as in the role of full-back and that has added to my experience. It has probably helped to further my international career too."

It certainly has. Not only has Staunton taken his collection of full caps beyond the seventy mark, but he has also skippered the side — a reflection of his growth as a player since he joined Villa. He has since moved on, a wiser and better player.

Paul McGrath has now retired, but what a player he was as Dwight Yorke explained.

"Macca was one of the best players I've ever worked with. There was no real weakness in his game. It was a shame that he was hampered for so long by the injuries he carried, but it was typical of him that he just carried on — almost as if they didn't exist. In his day I think he was one of the world's best defenders."

Few would argue with that, certainly not Dean Saunders who also rated him very highly.

"I never saw him have a bad game. He's probably the only player I have ever known who could play as well as he did without training. He hardly ever trained. He was the strongest man at the club when I was there and yet he was very shy. He has one of those faces that people could not fail to recognise, but he was never comfortable with that recognition."

In 1993 Paul McGrath was named PFA "Player of the Year", an award he richly deserved.

"Winning the award came as a bit of a surprise," he said. "I could think of other players who were performing better than me during that season. I actually voted for Paul Ince!"

McGrath joined Villa under something of a cloud. His relationship with his former Manchester United boss, Alex Ferguson, was not good. However, he shrugged off that episode of his career and dedicated himself to his new club despite constant worries about his knee problems.

"My knees were wearing out. It was not the way I wanted it to be but I had no real say in the matter. I don't really know what's wrong with them even now, but it could have been much worse. I wasn't going to start complaining about a couple of aching legs!"

He never did complain. Instead he proved himself as one of the best and most courageous defenders ever to pull on an Aston Villa shirt.

Gary Charles is the man who came back. He joined Villa from Derby County in January 1995, but injury saw him struggling to get into the side. Brian Little had plans for him though.

"I watched Gary Charles all season and found him to be an excellent user of the ball in a way which would make him an ideal wing-back. He was very confident, fast and effective, and that is why I encouraged him to play a very attack-minded full-back role in partnership with Steve Staunton."

The role fitted him so well that Gary Charles displaced Fernando Nelson, the Portuguese star who was previously playing for Bobby Robson at Sporting Lisbon.

Earl Barrett was also a popular defender with Villa for three years and proved himself a tough tackler and a flying winger. Mark Bosnich remembers him well.

"He was a good guy to have in front of you. He had a couple of nicknames at Villa. Some called him 'Grace Jones' because he looked a bit like her, others called him 'Dougie' — which is a club nickname for their pet thicko. He was a really nice bloke, quiet, but a consistently good player. I rarely saw anyone get the better of him."

Alan Wright has worn a Villa shirt proudly of late. Joining the club transformed his career, as he will tell you.

"When I was out injured for five months Blackburn bought Graeme Le Saux, and that meant that even when I returned to playing I would be in the Reserves. If I had stayed at Ewood Park I could possibly have got back into the side and won the championship with them, but as soon as I knew that Villa were interested in me I wanted to come here. I was told on the Thursday and I signed on the following day — that's how keen I was!

"It wasn't just that I wanted first-team football but that I knew Villa would be good for me. I was getting frustrated and stale at Blackburn. I knew that would not happen to me at Villa. We went through a bit of a bad patch when I joined but we had success in the Coca-Cola Cup and built on that. We have had our ups and downs since, but I believe that the stretch of the squad will see us in with a serious chance of major honours during the coming few seasons.

"For years I lived with schoolteachers, coaches, and everyone else telling me that I would never make it as a professional footballer because I simply wasn't big enough. They were all wrong! Blackpool was my first club and then I joined Blackburn before they got into the top division. Joining Villa

Joe Rutherford clears from a Charlton attack at The Valley in April 1939 with Villa's Massie and Callaghan watching. Rutherford joined Villa just before World War Two and was still there after it finished to provide a safe pair of hands, along with Alan Wakeman, as Villa moved into the 1950s.

Aston Villa pictured in 1949-50. Back row (left to right): H. Bourne (trainer), C. Gibson, J. Harrison, J. Rutherford, H. Parkes, F. Moss, C. Martin. Front row: W. Goffin, T. Ford, I. Powell, R. Dorsett, L. Smith.

Tommy Thompson gets a foot to the ball, challenged by Bolton's Higgins and Edwards at Villa Park during a First Division match in December 1951.

Aston Villa, 1952-53. Back row (left to right): H. Bourne (trainer), D. Blanchflower, H. Parkes, D. Parsons, F. Moss, P. Aldis. Front row: K. Roberts, T. Thompson, R. Dorsett, D. Walsh, J. Dixon, W. Goffin.

Peter Aldis and the legendary England centre-forward Tommy Lawton, then playing for Brentford, do battle during a fourth-round FA Cup replay at Griffin Park in March 1953.

George Martin, who managed Villa from December 1950 to August 1953. When he arrived at Villa Park he found a pressure-cooker atmosphere.

Jimmy Dugdale and goalkeeper Keith Jones make sure that Tottenham's Bobby Smith is no danger during a First Division game at White Hart Lane in January 1957.

Aston Villa, FA Cup winners in 1957, Back row (left to right): P. Aldis, S. Lynn, S. Crowther, N. Sims, J. Dugdale, D. Pace, T. Birch. Front row: Eric Houghton (manager), L. Smith, J. Sewell, W. Myerscough, J. Dixon, P. McParland, Billy Moore (trainer). On ground: P. Saward. Former player Eric Houghton "was Aston Villa", said Johnny Dixon.

Peter McParland, scorer of both Villa's goals at Wembley, and Manchester United's Duncan Edwards and stand-in goalkeeper Jackie Blanchflower watch the ball in the 1957 FA Cup Final.

Aston Villa, 1961-62. Back row (left to right): A. O'Neil, S. Lynn, J. Dugdale, N. Sims, D. Dougan, G. Lee, P. McParland. Front row: Joe Mercer (manager), R. Wylie, J. Neal, V. Crowe, J. MacEwan, R. Thomson, M. Shaw (trainer). On ground: H. Burrows, A. Deakin.

Ron Wylie tries a back header but West Ham's Martin Peters seems to have got there first. Tom Ewing is the No 11 in this League Cup-tie at Villa Park in October 1963.

Villa goalkeeper Colin Withers blocks a shot from Ian St John at Anfield in February 1967. Villa lost this First Division game 1-0 and seven days later went down by the same score on the same ground in the FA Cup. The combined attendance for the two games was nearly 100,000.

Relegated Villa at the start of the 1967-68 season. Back row (left to right): C. Aitken, J. Sleeuwenhoek, J. Woodward, C. Withers, L. Chatterley, D. Pountney, A. Deakin. Middle row: Tommy Cummings (manager), W. Anderson, G. Parker, B. Stobart, M. Tindall, P. Broadbent, J. MacLeod, W. Baxter (trainer). On ground: K. Bradley, A. Scott, M. Wright.

It just got worse! In August 1969 this Villa squad were on the brink of taking the club into the Third Division for the first time in its history. Back row (left to right): I. Hamilton, B. Hole, F. Turnbull, B. Lynch, K. Bradley. Middle row: L. Martin, D. Simmonds, E. Edwards, J. Dunn, N. Rioch, C. Aitken, D. Rudge. Front row: A. Cox (trainer), M. Wright, M. Ferguson, B. Tiler, B. Rioch, W. Anderson, Tommy Docherty (manager).

Tommy Docherty said, "I didn't admit it at the time but it broke my heart to leave Villa ...I was never happier than during my days at Villa Park."

Former Villa player Vic Crowe took over from The Doc and during his first summer began to turn the club around.

The Villa defence are devastated as Spurs' Martin Chivers opens the scoring against the Third Division club in the 1971 League Cup Final at Wembley.

In the 1960s Charlie Aitken was probably the star defender. He began his Villa career in 1961 and remained at the club until 1976, making more than 660 first-team appearances.

Ron Saunders – his appointment as Villa manager in June 1974 proved to be a major turning point in the club's history.

Chico Hamilton scores from the penalty spot in Villa's 6-1 hammering of Hartlepool United in the 1974-75 League Cup.

Villa's squad for the start of the 1976-77 season. Back row (left to right): C. Young, B. Little, S. Hunt, K. Mansfield, J. Deehan. Middle row: Roy MacLaren (first-team coach), K. Leonard, G. Smith, J. Burridge, A. Gray, J. Findlay, F. Carrodus, R. McDonald. Front row: R. Graydon, L. Phillips, J. Gidman, C. Nicholl, Ron Saunders (manager), J. Robson, D. Mortimer, I. Ross.

Andy Gray was undoubtedly one of Villa's all-time favourite strikers and is still held in the greatest esteem at the club.

Long-time Villa photographer Terry Weir caught the players in celebration with the League Cup after their epic 1977 Final tie against Everton.

Villa line up with the League Cup, ready for the 1977-78 season. Back row (left to right): C. Young, J. Findlay, J. Burridge, N. Spink, A. Evans, I. Linton. Middle row: Roy MacLaren (first-team coach), D. Evans, M. Buttress, J. Gregory, A. Gray, G. Smith, D. Hughes, G. Cowans, Peter Downs (physiotherapist). Front row: J. Deehan, A. Cropley, L. Phillips, J. Gidman, Ron Saunders (manager), J. Robson, B. Little, D. Mortimer, F. Carrodus.

Dennis Mortimer heads Villa's third goal against West Ham at Villa Park in March 1978. A great captain and midfield inspiration, Mortimer was one of the chief reasons for Villa's triumphs at the start of the 1980s.

Brian Little prepares for the challenge of Crystal Palace's Jim Cannon at Villa Park in October 1978. Little, capped by England, was quite a goalscorer in his days as a player with Villa.

Villa's Allan Evans takes the ball away from QPR's Stan Bowles during the League game at Loftus Road in September 1978. Evans was almost an ever-present when Villa won first the League championship and then the European Cup.

It's ours! Aston Villa lift the European Cup after their victory over Bayern Munich in Rotterdam in 1982.

Five full internationals in Villa strip. From left to right are: Steve Hunt, Allan Evans, Nigel Spink, Andy Gray and Steve Hodge, pictured in 1986.

Tony Barton took over the reins after Ron Saunders left, and steered Villa to a glorious European triumph. "I couldn't see the sense in making sweeping changes," he said later.

Terry Weir's superb shot of David Platt heading probably his most important goal for Villa – the only one of the game against Bradford City in May 1988, a goal which put the club on course to regaining its place in the top flight.

Peter Withe, scored the winner on a fantastic night in Rotterdam which saw Villa lift the European Cup.

Paul McGrath – "Macca was one of the best players I've ever worked with," says Dwight Yorke.

Ron Atkinson took over in July 1991. "We had a decent team but that was all – nothing to shout about," he said. His parting, though, was certainly acrimonious.

Tony Daley was at Villa Park for ten years as a player but before that he was also one of the lads who stood regularly at the Holte End.

Dean Saunders, seen here in action with Chris Fairclough of Leeds in September 1992. Once he linked with Atkinson he looked happier and more confident than for some time.

Dalian Atkinson celebrates putting Villa 1-0 ahead against Ipswich Town in the Coca-Cola Cup in December 1992. "There's no doubt in my mind that Deano and I were made for each other," he said.

Dwight Yorke, pictured here shortly after his League debut in 1990, is probably one of the most popular strikers of all time at Villa Park. He was discovered by the club while on tour in the West Indies. He was only 16 and still at school, but he was already an international for Trinidad and Tobago.

Ugo Ehiogu – rated highly by Dwight Yorke: "…good in the air …very quick …his tackling is especially good …he likes to score goals too." Here he is indulging in a bit of shirt-pulling with West Ham's John Hartson.

Gareth Southgate – "We think the world of the fans. I can honestly say that if the result of a game goes against us, we feel terrible for them."

Doug Ellis – a few times Villa has appeared to be terminally ill but has been saved by an emergency operation. "Deadly Doug" has proved to be a brilliant surgeon.

was quite different though. Here was a big club, already among the elite, prepared to spend money on buying me. That meant a lot to me and still does!"

Riccardo Scimeca is one of those players who sounds as if he has come from somewhere exotic — a part of the great foreign import drive — but in fact he was born in Leamington Spa and joined Villa straight from school as a trainee. He signed professional forms in July 1993 and has since proved what he can do as a central defender. His best days are yet to come — but come they will. Then there is another defender with an exotic name. Ugochuku Ehiogu is such a mouthful that Ron Atkinson labelled him 'Ugo' and that has been his name ever since. Like Scimeca he might sound as if he has travelled thousands of miles to play for Aston Villa, and yet he was born in Hackney and joined Villa from West Bromwich where he was a trainee.

Dwight Yorke rates him very highly.

"He is very good in the air and very quick on his feet. His tackling is especially good and, being a big man, he is excellent in the middle of the defence. He likes to score goals too."

In fact Ugo doesn't just like to score goals — he LOVES to score goals!

"I sometimes stay behind for extra practice with Mark Bosnich and one or two of the others because I love putting the ball into the back of the net. I used to play up front when I was a kid. Now I only go forward if we have a situation that calls for it. There were a lot of people who said I didn't have what it takes but, thanks to Villa, I haven't done too badly. I have played for England at senior level and I have a few medals. Hopefully I shall have a few more before long."

And so say all of us!

CHAPTER NINE

IN THE MIDDLE OF THINGS

THEY used to call them half-backs or inside-forwards, but today they fall into the category of midfielders. They are probably the fittest and hardest-working players on the park, fitting into the defence and the attack as needed. Eric Cantona once described them as 'the water carriers', which is quite an apt description since they are indeed the dynamos of the engine, the work-horses on the battlefield, who have more than their fair share of the toil but probably not as much of the glory as they deserve.

Immediately after the war, Eddie Lowe was one of the most outstanding wing-halves at the club, although he probably became even more famous when he was later transferred to Fulham in 1950. His brother, Reg, also played for Villa and also joined Fulham. Their father, Arthur, had been a goalkeeper with Villa between the wars.

Harry Parkes played both alongside him and against him.

"Eddie was a character. He was a very good player who always looked older than his years and used to get some stick from the crowd because of his hair loss. You couldn't, however, take away from him the fact that he was an energetic player who was good at both passing and laying on the perfect pass. He also had tremendous stamina and would be ready for another hour's play when the rest of us had had enough."

In the early 1950s there came another star — the legendary Danny Blanchflower. Yes, Danny Blanchflower was a legend. No other word would be anywhere near adequate. He had been playing for Barnsley and was already a Northern Ireland international when he joined Villa in March 1951. Prior to that he had been playing for Glentoran and was a graduate of St Andrew's University. Why was he so special? Probably because of his excellent brain, his determination to win and his undoubted leadership qualities.

Probably Villa never saw the best of him because he left in October 1954 and became a Tottenham player destined to create history.

Johnny Dixon was one of his team-mates.

"Danny was a marvellous player. He became better and better as the years went by, but even when he was with us he had something about him that was quite unique. He was not the most skillful footballer you would ever find but he was competent in all he did. His real talent was his mind. He could see things long before they happened, he could demolish the opposition defence with just one unexpected pass. It took the rest of us a while to get on the same wavelength so you can imagine how difficult he made it for the opposition. It was almost comical at times because part of his job was to mark an opponent, but he never needed to. They were so worried about him that he would always have one or two watching him!"

There was some temporary ill-feeling when Blanchflower left the club. He had requested a transfer because, as he saw it, "The Villa, while a fine club who treated their players well, lived too much in the past, which meant that the team lacked inspiration and hope for better football."

Nevertheless, Blanchflower always had a soft spot for Villa and enjoyed his later visits to Villa Park as a player, a journalist and a speaker at club functions. On a personal note, I often sat next to him in the press box at various grounds and on more than one occasion when Villa were involved he said, rather wistfully, "I used to play for them you know. Nice club!"

One of his favourite mottoes was, "It's not the size of the man in the fight but the size of the fight in the man." He lived by that.

Jackie Sewell had a happy four years at Villa after he joined in December 1955 for £20,000. He had previously been Britain's most expensive player when he was sold by Notts County to Sheffield Wednesday just four years earlier for £34,500. He began his career as a goalscorer but during his Villa days he was considered to be even more dangerous as a play maker.

"He was a very influential inside-right," said Johnny Dixon. "Jackie was another very clever player who could win a game for you with just one pass. He knew all about scoring too. He was an England international and you could see why. He had class. He could beat players, hold the play up, create chances, help in defence. Jackie was a good all-rounder and he was brilliant with both feet. Jackie was an intelligent player like Danny Blanchflower and he had a great understanding of the game."

Pat Saward was around at the same time and, like Jackie

Sewell, was a member of the 1957 FA Cup-winning side. Saward preferred the No 6 shirt but he was equally at home as an attacking inside-left, or a deeper left-half.

"Pat was an Irish international because of his parents," explained Johnny Dixon. "He was actually born in London and came to Villa from Millwall. As I remember, he scored on his Villa debut. We were at home to Manchester United and it was quite a game because we drew 4-4. It was some debut that he had but I think he enjoyed it. He stayed for several years so it couldn't have put him off!"

Pat Saward became captain of Villa for a while but in 1961 he moved on to Huddersfield, and later went into coaching and management.

When Alan Deakin made his debut in December 1959, he was handed Pat Saward's No 6 shirt — a shirt he was to wear for much of the next ten years.

"I was one of Joe Mercer's boys at the start and I played under five different managers. It was a bit like having five different jobs one after the other because they all had their own expectations and styles of play. It was a good experience for me. I had joined Villa from school and had all the usual cleaning jobs to do before I was allowed near a football. Later, I captained the side for a season, which was something I had dreamed about since being a kid. I had always loved the Villa and to become skipper was the ultimate for me.

"There were some excellent players at the club during my time and, even though we suffered relegation, we still had our moments. I still keenly follow Villa!"

As Deakin faded from the Villa scene in 1970, Pat McMahon was just coming to life. They were club-mates for a year and then McMahon's career took off.

Pat McMahon was not a midfielder until he joined Aston Villa. In fact he was almost not a full-time professional footballer at all, even though he had performed for several seasons with Celtic. Let him explain.

"Joining Villa made a big difference to my life and especially when Vic Crowe was manager. You could say that he helped me to find myself. I was a Celtic fan as a kid but I never really thought that I might end up with a career in the game myself — especially since I was training to be a priest throughout most of my teen years. I still used to kick a ball about behind the monastery. I spent seven years like that and then, when I was nineteen, I realised that I could not go through with it and I abruptly ended my studies.

"There was a lot of questioning from various people and the pressure was getting to me a little so I packed a bag, grabbed my guitar and went to the continent to have a look around Europe. I lived rough for some months before coming back to Britain and working as a labourer on building sites. At least it kept me fit and, back in Scotland, I became centre-forward for Kilsyth Rangers, one of the junior clubs.

"When I took a job with the Post Office in London, it meant that I could no longer play for Kilsyth. They went on a Cup run though and asked me if I would fly back to play for them if they paid the air-fares. As it turned out, we went right through to the Final and attracted the attention of several professional clubs. I was approached by Celtic.

"I joined them and went straight into the first team. I felt that I had done well during my debut games but Jock Stein had other ideas and I soon found myself kicking my heels in the Reserves. We had a row about it and Jock told me that he didn't like my attitude. He was probably right, although I didn't think so at the time. At the end of the season I was given a free transfer but I did not have to wait long for another club. Tommy Docherty was manager of Aston Villa at the time and he decided to take a chance on me.

"The Doc did not mince his words, he simply said, 'I think you can play a bit, but I'm taking a risk. I'm willing to back my judgement if you are willing to work at the game.' He played me as an out-and-out striker but, on reflection, I was not really competitive enough and it was just a bit of a game to me. I had not yet come to terms with being a professional. I still thought of Saturday afternoon as a bit of fun.

"I had a lot of time for Tommy Docherty, he genuinely had the interests of Aston Villa at heart — but Vic Crowe proved to be the man to improve my game. He was always quietly spoken but very direct, and I remember having a really long heart-to-heart with him in his office. It was the longest face-to-face talk I have ever had, before or since. He told me that I lacked competitiveness and that I never tried to win the ball. 'To play brilliantly when you have the ball is not enough,' he told me. 'You have to play off the ball and try to win it.' He was right, and he had summed up my game better than anyone. He stopped me playing as a striker and put me in midfield. It gave me a completely different outlook and changed my attitude instantly — and as a bonus, I began to enjoy my football even more.

"My highlights of being at Villa were winning the Third Division championship and playing at Wembley in the League Cup Final in 1971. Even though we lost 2-0 to Tottenham it was still a great experience. Another of my favourite memories was playing against Santos in a friendly at Villa Park. Pele played and we beat them 2-1. I scored one of our goals.

"We had some great players at the time and it is amazing

that we had sunk to the old Third Division. When you consider that during my time there were players like the Rioch brothers, Bruce and Neil, George Curtis, Chico Hamilton, Jim Cumbes and many other top men, it is incomprehensible that we were not among the challengers for the League championship.

"I left Villa in 1976 and went to America to play for Portland Timbers first of all, and later for Caribous of Colorado, finally finishing up with Atlanta. I liked America and have since settled down as a partner in a firm supplying aluminium, but I still pick up the Villa results and keep up with all the Villa Park news. I grew up at Aston Villa and have very happy memories of my time there."

It was often said that Pat McMahon had only one pace — very fast! He certainly brought forth a roar of approval, expectation and excitement every time he had the ball at his feet — and he scored some vital goals during his years in the claret and blue. Tommy Docherty had baked the McMahon cake — and Vic Crowe had certainly added the icing!

Around the same time, Ian 'Chico' Hamilton was also making a name for himself. A teenage sensation when he was transferred from Southend for £40,000, he stayed until Sheffield United signed him in the summer of 1976.

"We had some good times during my Villa days. We were Third Division champions and twice reached the Final of the League Cup at Wembley. We won one of the games and I still have the medal. There were a lot of young players at Villa at the time and you could see that the club was moving in the right direction."

Villa moved from the Third to the First Division during 'Chico' Hamilton's period with the club and he played an important part in that success, as Ian Ross explained.

"Chico was a very fast, talented player who dazzled opposition defenders. He was always full of life and proved to be a great goal provider. He never seemed to get tired."

Talking about Ian Ross, he wore the No 6 shirt for five busy seasons, making more than 200 first-team appearances in a comparatively short time. For many of those games he was captain of the side. A Scotsman, he had started his soccer at Liverpool under the scrutiny of Bill Shankly who admired Ross, even though he did allow Villa to buy him for £70,000 in 1972.

"It was difficult to get regular first-team football at Anfield in those days, especially as a midfield player, because the place was bursting with talent and Bill Shankly liked to make as few changes to his team as possible. It gave me a big lift when I joined Villa, a terrific club. I certainly did not see it as a downward step. Villa has always been a big club to me."

Ian Ross had a very successful spell at Villa Park, with two promotions and a League Cup win. He left in December 1976, but returned a few years later for a brief period as a coach before going overseas on coaching assignments.

It was Ron Saunders who saw John Robson's potential as a midfield player. It was generally accepted that Robson, who had been signed by Vic Crowe from Derby for £90,000 at the end of 1972, was a defender. Ron Saunders had other ideas.

"He just told me to do my best and he had given me some midfield work in training. I had no problem in making the switch though — I found that I enjoyed the extra freedom it gave me. My memories of Villa include the League Cup Finals, promotion, and those wonderful supporters".

It was unfortunate that Robson's career was cut short by multiple sclerosis in 1977.

Leighton Phillips was a Villa star of the late 1970s. He could play just about anywhere on the pitch, but his Villa career saw him specialising as an inside-forward, as Jimmy Rimmer recalled.

"Clever player — I knew him before the Villa days and he was always very talented. He was quick-thinking as well as quick-footed. He could play as a full-back, a centre-half, a striker, and just about anywhere else. I'm sure that he would have pinched my job if it had been available. He played an important part in getting Villa back into the First Division."

Gordon 'Sid' Cowans has had three different spells at Villa — two as a player and more recently as a member of the coaching staff.

"My first time at Villa began in July 1974. I was a fifteen-year-old apprentice at first but, under the management of Ron Saunders, I made good progress and even before I signed as a full professional I had made my League debut. We went on to win the championship and the European Cup and then, in 1985, Paul Rideout and myself were sold to Bari of Italy. It was all very exciting, the prospect of playing in Italy, but it didn't last!

"Everything went well for the first season, until the last part when Bari were relegated and suddenly my continental dream had turned sour. For the next two years I felt that I was being buried in the obscurity of Italian Second Division football. It hurt me that people back home were also forgetting all about me. Consequently, I spent virtually all of those two years trying to get back to England. Queen's Park Rangers made a try for me but Bari refused to do business.

"In the end it took the finish of my contract to pave the way for my return to Villa. It had been an horrendous time, worse even than when I suffered a double fracture of my right leg in a pre-season tournament in 1983. I wanted to return to Villa but

I was concerned that the fans might expect the same Gordon Cowans of six or seven years earlier when we were winning everything. I couldn't be sure that I would be able to live up to the fans' expectations.

"Graham Taylor was boss by then and he wasn't put off and convinced me that it would be all right. I also realised how much it would mean for my family to return to their old surroundings in the Midlands. When the move was finally made I experienced a tremendous feeling of relief. Suddenly I felt that I had really come home to Aston Villa."

Cowans stayed at Villa Park for just over three years before leaving to see out his playing career elsewhere. However, now he is back and a part of the coaching team, perhaps adding something of the style once described by Andy Gray, who said, "Gordon has everything a top midfielder should have — pace, skill, power, tackling ability, vision and confidence. No wonder he has had such an outstanding career for club and country."

Frank Carrodus spent five years in the Villa midfield, a tremendously powerful player who seemed able to keep going without stopping for a breather for the full ninety minutes and then some. In 200 appearances for the club he played a great part in Villa's return to the First Division and in two League Cup victories. Frank later played for Birmingham City for a while. Des Bremner was another of those rare species who played for both Birmingham City and Villa, but his best years were undoubtedly in the claret and blue. He was a right-sided midfielder who relished all-out attack and had learned his trade in his native Scotland with Hibernian. Having joined Villa in 1979 he was also a member of that exclusive side of the championship and European Cup era.

Dennis Mortimer is another of Villa's legends. A great captain and midfield inspiration who was one of the chief reasons for Villa's triumphs at the start of the 1980s. Tony Morley was without doubt one of the most exciting wingers ever to pull on a Villa shirt. Today he would probably find himself straying inside rather more but, in the time of Ron Saunders and Tony Barton, Morley was a classic winger.

"The fans loved him," said Peter Withe. "Whenever he had the ball at his feet they would roar him on. He is one of the best providers I have ever seen. He was very fast but always kept great control, and he put in some wonderful crosses. He was more than capable of scoring goals himself and made a huge contribution to every game."

Tony Daley followed in the same mould, although his own inspiration was Mark Walters.

"I used to watch him before I became a Villa player and he was my hero. I used to love seeing him get the ball and take on defenders. He would have them going this way and that before leaving them for dead as he sprinted off with the ball. I always wanted to play like that. I thought he was just brilliant and he certainly inspired me to work hard at ball skills."

Walters, a local lad, joined Villa from school and became the replacement for Tony Morley. His Villa career was terrific but he went on to even greater things with Glasgow Rangers and Liverpool. Many fans think that his continued presence at Villa Park would have made a huge difference to the club's fortunes.

Tony Daley did indeed go on to emulate his hero, both in ability and in success. An England international, like Walters, Daley's only real problem was injuries.

"It was great to be a Villa player. Just making my debut made all my dreams come true, but what happened later made it all the more magical. I never expected to play for England and all that came as a big bonus. I have Graham Taylor to thank for that. He made a tremendous difference to my career both at Villa and when he was England manager."

Once again we find ourselves with an apparently endless list of great players who have been defending or attacking midfielders, goal providers par excellence, all of whom have worn the Villa shirt. Shaun Teale, Derek Mountfield, Kevin Richardson, Martin Keown, Steve McMahon, Ray Houghton, Andy Townsend and Steve Hodge are among them.

Today, Mark Draper is maintaining the tradition of Villa midfielders. Brian Little signed him from Leicester and considered him to be one of his best buys.

"Mark was a great signing, a terrific player, a guy who wanted to play for Aston Villa, a guy who wanted to be the best and be in among the best. He likes to have the ball, has a good passing range, is good on the ball and can even score goals. He has the desire to be the best midfield player in the country. In the 1960s and 70s every team had a player like Mark Draper, but now he is one of an endangered species."

Draper himself is still full of ambition and has a strong belief that Villa are on the threshold of being a major force during the coming years.

"We have been a nearly club for several seasons, but I really feel that we are close to being the best in the country. The squad has come together in the last year or so and there has been a lot of hard work put in. I am convinced that we are on the verge of something big."

There is another extremely talented midfielder at Villa Park in the shape of Ian Taylor, who has been a revelation since he joined from Sheffield Wednesday in December 1994. Another local lad, Taylor will play anywhere but his place behind the strikers has proved to be most deadly. Not only is he a great provider and a very capable goalscorer but he has another talent that is not so readily observed during a game, as Mark Draper revealed.

"Ian is the main joker in the dressing-room. he just never stops cracking jokes and doing impressions. He'll do anybody and everybody. His repertoire of television stars is amazing. He's like Harry Enfield — only better!"

The dressing-room atmosphere is so important — but then, so is good coaching and the right attitude. In that department there is one midfielder who was not only a star at Villa Park but went on to become internationally famous with great performances for his country, whom he captained. He also achieved fame as being the most expensive footballer in the world. We are talking of course about David Platt.

David's rejection by Manchester United and career-saving tuition at Crewe have been well chronicled, but he was certainly an inspiration at Villa and played a major part in Graham Taylor's revival of the club's fortunes.

"There is no doubt that I have had a great career and some wonderful experiences," said David. "I owe much to a lot of people. Probably I owe most to Aston Villa and the club's supporters. They took a chance on me when I was at Crewe and turned me into an England international. It was a big wrench for me when I left Villa Park and I still keenly look for Villa's results. I want to see them winning things. When I first joined the club I became something of a fan — and I still am!"

Brian Little called midfielders an endangered species. With many clubs employing the tactics of a big boot upfield to launch an attack, he is probably right. In some games midfielders have become little more than ball-boys, fetching and carrying anything that goes astray. At Villa though, the midfielders are appreciated, and Villa Park has become quite a sanctuary over the years for those players who have more to offer than boot and bustle. Long may that continue.

CHAPTER TEN

STRIKERS

T O THE winner goes the spoils, to the striker goes the glory. There is no doubt that if you are a youngster seeking the spotlight you really ought to be aiming to become a goalscorer. They are the men who get all the fuss when things go right. They used to be known as centre-forwards of course — usually big blokes with heads like hammers, feet like power drills and elbows like chisels. Villa have been well-blessed during the last half-century with a wide variety of such men.

Trevor Ford was probably the first of the post-war scoring superstars. A Welsh international centre-forward of the old school, he fell into a dispute with his club, Swansea, and Villa snapped him up for £9,500.

"I went to a cinema when all this was going on. I was a Swansea player when I went in and an Aston Villa player when I came out," he recalled. He remained a Villa player for nearly four years and scored 61 goals in 128 first-team appearances.

"It was a big club and I was delighted to sign from Swansea. It was all a bit strange for me at first because I had only played for Clapton Orient outside of Wales — and that was as a war-time guest. I was taken aback by the sheer size of the place when

I went to Villa Park, but everyone encouraged me and I was confident that I could do well."

Sailor Brown played alongside him.

"He was a lovely player, a typical centre-forward who knew no fear. He had a great first touch and could score from any angle. He looked after himself and he was always very fit. I think he missed Wales a bit at first and it took him a little while to settle. He didn't, perhaps, get the best of service because there were so many changes going on in the side at that time, and I think he got a bit fed-up in the end and moved on to Sunderland. But he was a great player, a tremendous goalscorer and became quite a football legend."

For each of his full seasons at Villa, Ford was top scorer. When he left in October 1950, Dave Walsh was signed as his successor from West Bromwich. The Welshman was replaced by an Irishman who was also a proven goalscorer. Johnny Dixon remembers him well.

"He was not one of those centre-forwards who just closed their eyes and hit anything that came near them. He was very good at sharing the chances. He was a regular scorer but he would also lay on chances for other people and he had a hand in at least as many goals as he scored."

Of course there were other goal scorers around at the time, Derek Pace for one. He had scored on his debut against Burnley in March 1951 and made a valuable contribution to the Villa goalscoring during the 1950s — as did Peter McParland of course. Then there was the late, lamented Gerry Hitchens, another of Villa's legends.

"I remember Gerry well," said Johnny Dixon. "Who could ever forget him? He was a marvellous chap. When he first joined Villa he was a military policeman so he knew how to handle things if the going got tough. He had to finish his National Service before he could fully concentrate on his football with the Villa, but he already had quite a reputation for scoring goals.

"He certainly scored some goals when he came to Villa. His most memorable match was when he scored five goals in a slaughtering of Charlton at Villa Park. Villa won 11-1. The following week he got a hat-trick in a 5-0 win at Bristol City. We won the Second Division that season of 1959-60. The following year he was on form again and helped Villa get to the League Cup Final, but then he left to take a big contract in Italy with Inter-Milan. The supporters were shocked. They thought the world of him, he was their biggest hero of the time and suddenly he was gone. He was a fantastic goalscorer though. They don't come along like him very often!"

Derek Dougan had a couple of seasons with Villa after Joe Mercer signed him as a replacement for Gerry Hitchens. Villa fans probably never saw the best of him although he did score 26 goals in 60 games. Within a few weeks of joining Villa he was the centre of controversy. A couple of reporters stumbled across him dressed in tattered kit and with his head completely bald. Needless to say, their reports were not exactly flattering and did little to enhance the respectable Villa image. A nagging injury spoiled his time at Villa but one thing is for sure, he has never been forgotten.

Tony Hateley was another of the great Villa goalscorers. From 1963 to 1967 he hit home 86 goals in 148 appearances, many of which came from his head. He was so prolific with headed goals that it was once said that he even took penalties with his head! To the Villa fans it didn't matter whether he scored the goals with his head or his backside as long as he got them over the line.

One of Villa's most popular strikers was Andy Lochhead, who only stayed for just over three seasons but made an immense impression. Just to give some idea of how the Villa fans felt about him, he returned a few years later as coach of Oldham and was given a standing ovation by the entire crowd. What was so special about him? Vic Crowe, the manager who signed him early in 1970, explained:

"It was his huge contribution to every game and to the club itself. During a match he never stopped battling. He never shirked anything and he inspired everyone around him. He made a major contribution to getting the club out of the Third Division and to the 1971 League Cup Final. All the young players who were here at the time looked up to him, and he helped every one of them."

Brian Little remembers the inspiration he gained from Andy Lochhead.

"He was a giant! — My hero! He was the sort of player we all wanted to be like. You only had to watch him for a few minutes to want to copy his attitude. He was never too busy to help everyone else either. All the lads picked up tips from him. Andy was No 1 to us."

When Little made his debut at the end of the 1971-72 season, Lochhead scored in a 5-1 thumping of Torquay at Villa Park. Brian Little scored one of the other goals.

"Andy was brilliant. He gave you confidence, and the fact that I came off the pitch feeling ten feet tall was really down to the help that I had been given by him."

That season Andy Lochhead finished with a total of 25 League goals as Villa won the Third Division title.

"It was a great season but it was a great club too," said Andy himself. "There was really no valid reason why such a big club should have slipped down the League like that. The supporters were marvellous and I was deeply touched when they gave me such a welcome a few years later. My Villa days were certainly happy ones."

Dixie Dean, the legendary superstar striker of Everton in the 1930s, never played for Aston Villa — but John 'Dixie' Deehan did! He was a local lad whom Villa had watched several times as a schoolboy but could not make up their minds about — that is until Arsenal attempted to take him on trial.

"The Villa scouts told my dad that if I went down to London for trials I would never come back. Arsenal would easily persuade me that Highbury was the place for me. I don't think my parents fancied the idea of me being near the bright lights of London when I was so young. Needless to say, a month's trial at Villa Park was quickly arranged. I was only there for a week before they signed me as an apprentice. I was thrilled to bits. The nickname was nothing to do with my scoring ability but was just because my surname sounded like Dean.

"I never regretted joining Villa. I was at Villa Park for five years after signing senior professional forms in 1974 and during that time I had some great moments — as well as one or two I would probably rather forget. I learned a great deal, especially about how you can be a villain and a hero all in the space of a few moments. I remember a game against Ipswich which we won 6-1. Andy Gray was in great form but one of his attempts hit the crossbar and came straight to me. The goal was wide open but somehow I headed it over. I couldn't believe it — and neither could anyone else. Within a few minutes we were on the attack again, and when the cross came over I jumped above everyone else and headed a really difficult one straight into the net. It taught me that you cannot dwell on mistakes or they will ruin your game and any other chances that might come your way.

"On the brighter side I had some great experiences with Villa, both in domestic and European games. I won seven England Under-23 caps and I was called up for the senior squad — although I never got any further than the bench. Even so, it was a great honour to be involved. A lot of people told me that I should have elected to play for the Republic of Ireland. I would have qualified because of my parentage and I had done a lot of work with the Irish clubs around Birmingham, so I felt quite at home with Irish people. I was even presented with a set of golf clubs as a token for some of the charity work that I had been doing, and they got Johnny Giles to present it. He asked me about playing for the Republic but my boss, Ron Saunders, told me that he believed I would be playing for England seniors one day — so I stuck with England.

"My greatest honour with Villa was winning the League Cup in 1977. We had a terrific tussle with Everton which went two replays. The first game at Wembley ended in a 0-0 draw and, to be fair, it was not a good game for the spectators. The second match was at Hillsborough and this one finished at 1-1. Finally it was settled at Old Trafford where we won 3-2 after extra-time. We were happy to receive our medals but I think we were also relieved that it was all over!

"I won further honours with Norwich City later on, but that League Cup medal which I gained with Villa has pride of place among my collection of souvenirs."

Andy Gray was undoubtedly one of Villa's all-time favourite strikers and is still held in the greatest esteem at the club. The circumstances in which he joined Villa are indelibly marked in his memory as he thought that he was being dropped by his Dundee United boss and not actually being transferred.

"It was in the early part of the 1975-76 season and, to be honest, I was not having a particularly good run. I was 20 years old and had only been a professional for a couple of years. Our manager was Jim McLean and I can remember that he seemed a little distant on this one particular day — a Friday I believe. Usually he would stop and have a general chat but on this occasion he actually seemed to be avoiding me. We were due to play away to Celtic the next day and when we were in Glasgow I always stayed overnight at my mother's home. I was born in Glasgow and she still lived there. As I was leaving Tannadice, Jim McLean asked where he could contact me if he needed to speak to me later. I told him, of course, and remember thinking that he would be phoning me later to tell me that I had been dropped for the game. It wasn't at all like him as he would always speak to you face to face, but I convinced myself that I was out of the team for a game that I was very keen to play in. I was naturally very disappointed.

"Before I went to my mother's place I visited a girlfriend in Glasgow. I had only been there a few minutes when the phone rang. It was my mother, telling me to phone the club immediately. I was fully prepared for the worst and my suspicions seemed to be confirmed when Jim McLean said, 'I don't think you'll be playing against Celtic tomorrow.' Before I had the chance to ask the reason why, he continued, 'Because we've agreed terms with Aston Villa. If you are interested, be at Glasgow Airport in two hours!'

"I couldn't think of anything to say. One minute I thought I was being dropped and the next I was being given the chance to join one of England's most famous clubs. My biggest problem was that, just five days earlier, Schalke 04 of Germany had also made me a very attractive offer. They had been very hospitable and I could not have asked for a better deal. I wasn't sure that I was ready for such a major move but it was a very difficult proposition to refuse. That evening I travelled down to Birmingham for a meeting on the following day. I didn't sleep a wink all night. I kept asking myself the same question over and over again — 'What shall I do?'

"The following morning I met Ron Saunders and he made my mind up for me. He reminded me of Jim McLean and I knew that I would be able to get along with him. They were very much two of a kind — honest, direct, and ambitious for their club. I signed that morning and in the rush I even forgot to tell my mother. The first she heard about it was when my face appeared on television.

"Naturally I did not regret the move. I might have earned more money in Germany but I am convinced that Schalke could not have given me the satisfaction that I gained with Villa. My first-team debut was a League Cup-tie with Manchester United and I was overwhelmed with the crowd at Villa Park. However, I scored on that debut and that soon settled me."

What followed were four happy years at Villa Park, followed by another couple of years when he rejoined the club in 1985.

"I have great memories of my two spells at Villa. We won the League Cup and we had some great matches in the First Division and in Europe. On a personal note I was both 'PFA Player of the Year' and 'Young Player of the Year' in 1977. I don't think that has ever happened before or since and it is a tremendously humbling experience when your fellow pros vote for you like that. Villa players were banned from going to the London Hilton for the dinner and awards as we were in the League Cup Final replay with Everton. Special arrangements had to be made and the television cameras came to my house. A few of the Villa lads came along too and I received the awards in my own front room.

"As for goals, well there have been a few. Scoring the only goal of the game against Wolves on the opening day of the 1978-79 season was very special because it was a local derby game with nearly 44,000 at Villa Park. That win set us up for a pretty good season. Before that there had been a high scoring season for me in the 1976-77 campaign. We finished fourth in the table and I scored 25 goals in 36 League matches, which is probably why I was given the awards by the PFA. I scored hat-tricks against Ipswich and West Bromwich that season and there were also quite a few occasions when I scored two. Probably the best was against Liverpool at Villa Park a week or so before Christmas. I think the way we played in the first half of that game would have seen the destruction of just about any team in the world.

"Liverpool fielded a strong team with Kevin Keegan, Emlyn Hughes, Ray Clemence, Ian Callaghan and their other top players all in the side. I scored after nine minutes when John Robson put over a beautiful cross and I headed it past Ray Clemence. Two minutes later John Deehan added a second and then a third, and then Brian Little made it 4-0. Liverpool scored through Ray Kennedy but then Dennis Mortimer took a corner from the left and gave me the chance to head home our fifth. If Ray Clemence had not been in good form I am sure we could have run to double figures. It was a great game for us — definitely one for the scrap-book!"

During the Ron Atkinson era, Andy Gray returned as coach. Today of course, he is best known for his work with BskyB's football coverage, but his heart is still in the Midlands.

"I'm still as Scottish as ever, but I consider the Midlands to be my home. I love being here and I certainly don't regret turning down the chance to go to Germany on that fateful Friday in September 1975."

David Geddis joined Villa from Ipswich in 1979 with the unenviable task of filling the No 9 shirt vacated the previous season by Andy Gray.

"I was very happy to sign when Villa came in for me. They had a young side with several new faces and a lot of ambition. Taking over from Andy Gray didn't worry me. I knew he had been very popular but fans have to accept players in their own right. What did bother me was taking so long to get off the mark. When I scored my first goal it was a huge relief.

"Brian Little and I built up an understanding fairly quickly. We complemented each other. He had the close control and flair while I provided the hustle and bustle. I loved my time at Villa, a big club in every sense of the word — the stadium and set-up, the fans, everything was geared for success. It was great!"

Brian Little himself was quite a goalscorer during his playing days at Villa, which extended from 1969 when he joined the club as an apprentice to 1981 when his playing days were prematurely ended by injury. During that time he was also capped by England as a striker, which gives some idea that he was not at Villa just to make up the numbers! However, there is another side to Brian Little that you won't find in the record books.

"I was on my honeymoon when I was called up for England. What a choice! Heather and I continued our honeymoon later. Actually, as a player I was the most temperamental so-and-so you would ever find. I was terrible at times. I resented being told what to do if I felt it was of no benefit. I was something of a pain in the backside. Once I was told to cut my hair. I didn't think it would make me a better player so I packed my bags and went home."

As a Villa fan, striker Stan Collymore has had his own special heroes. They also, of course, were strikers who wore the claret and blue with honour.

"Gary Shaw and Peter Withe were my heroes, and Peter was at Villa Park when I arrived as a player. It was really weird when I met up with him after having idolised him as a kid."

Peter Withe had something to prove when he joined Villa in May 1980. His career up to that point had been something of a roller-coaster ride and while he had confidence in his own ability he seemed to have collected a posse of critics despite an impressive record.

"Looking back on my playing career, I'm surprised that I made it at all," he said. "There is no doubt that Aston Villa was the best thing that ever happened to me. Up to then I seemed to be travelling down a road that was full of holes — and I was falling into almost every one of them! I began at Southport in August 1971. Alec Baker signed me on amateur forms and told me he would make me a professional when I was 20 and had completed my apprenticeship as an electrician. Two months later he was sacked and I was looking for another club. I wrote to most of the Lancashire clubs but only Preston offered me a trial. I played for their reserves and then they told me that they would not be signing me.

"A month later I went on trial to Barrow but was offered the chance to go to South Africa instead to play for Port Elizabeth City. I had about ten days to sell up in Liverpool and take my wife and our young son to South Africa. We arrived with about £30 to our name. I had a factory job arranged by the club and had to train most evenings. After ten months the club folded and we were back to square one — only this time thousands of miles from home.

"We had originally planned to spend two years in South Africa so, when I was offered the chance to play alongside Derek Dougan at Arcadia Shepherds we accepted — even though we really wanted to come back home. It was through Dougan that I joined Wolves in November 1973, but again the silver lining was hiding a black cloud. I could not establish myself in the first team and, in April 1974, the club released me.

"America was calling and I joined Portland Timbers. There were several well-known names from English football in the States and I didn't do myself any harm by scoring 17 goals in 25 games. It prompted Birmingham manager, Freddie Goodwin, to fly out to see me and sign me for £40,000. At last it seemed that something was going right. Four games after my debut for the Blues, Freddie Goodwin was sacked and Willie Bell took over. He didn't really rate me and I kicked my heels for a year until I was on the move again.

"Nottingham Forest were next and Brian Clough and Peter Taylor were plotting the club's progress out of the Second Division. That was in September 1976 when I joined. In that first season we won the Anglo-Scottish Cup, my first-ever trophy as a professional, and promotion. In the second season we won the League championship and the League Cup. This was more like it. Unfortunately a pay dispute followed and I was transferred to Newcastle where I spent two disappointing seasons with a club that was struggling to stay in the Second Division. I could have wept for the supporters.

"So, by the time Villa came in for me at the end of the 1979-80 season I was really keen to prove to everyone that I was a good player who was worth more than the minefield that I had just been through. There were several clubs interested but the then Villa boss, Ron Saunders, convinced me that Villa would be the right choice. He was right of course!

"I joined in May 1980 and it just felt right. Ron Saunders had said that I was the last piece in his jigsaw and I really felt that Villa was on the threshold of great things. I said so to the press at the time. I had had a good spell at Forest but there were those who said that I had been lucky and I really wanted to prove them all wrong. Villa was the perfect club for me to do that."

Peter Withe's achievements with Villa are now history — and remarkable history too! Ron Saunders was delighted, he had spent his £200,000 wisely.

"I thought he could do a job for us and he proved us both right," said Ron. "He was a very good goalscorer. Given the right service and left to do the job he would deliver. He did deliver!"

Peter Withe began to deliver in his third game in Villa colours. His debut had been in a 2-1 away win at Leeds. Then came a home win over Norwich. The third game was at Manchester City and he scored twice to earn Villa a point. By the end of the season he was top scorer and Villa were champions.

"It was my second League championship and proved that the medal I had won at Forest was no fluke. We had been quietly confident all season but we had played it down so that we kept our concentration. The service from Tony Morley had been great and was a major factor in the goals scored by Gary Shaw and myself.

"I made my England debut that year and the following season we won the European Cup. I knew it was a wise move to join Villa, it made a huge difference to my career. In 1982 I had the honour of being in the England World Cup squad. I don't know if I would have been there if I had not had the chance to prove myself at Villa.

"I was sorry to leave the club in 1986 even though I went on to have a good spell with Sheffield United. I was drawn to Villa like a magnet though and when I had the chance to return to the club as assistant to Josef Venglos, and then again later as coach, I felt like I was coming home. The Villa shirt means everything to me and whatever happens in the future, my greatest memories will always be of scoring goals while wearing the shirt of that great club."

In 1987 Villa signed another crack shot. He came from Glasgow Rangers and he stayed for two seasons before going on to Bayern Munich. During that time he scored 25 Villa goals in 69 games. There were many who would like Alan McInally to have stayed much longer.

It is not possible to talk about Villa strikers without including Stan Collymore who has already explained his love-affair with the club. To those who have known him since childhood, he is the reality of a dream come true because he made it from the terraces on to the pitch.

"Every time I score a Villa goal it means so much more because I still remember the days when I used to leap up in the air when someone else was doing the scoring. There is only one thing better than celebrating someone else's Villa goal and that is scoring your own. I have never been one for setting targets at the beginning of each season because that way you never get disappointed — and sometimes you just have to spend more time as a provider than a goalscorer. I just go out there to try and play well in every game — and hopefully score too. I know that when you carry the 'striker' label you are expected to score

20 plus goals a season, but I never worry about that. If the team are playing well I know there will be goals and I'll get my share."

Stan Collymore can remember his favourite Villa goal.

"It was away to Tottenham at the end of August 1997. We had got off to a terrible start to the season. We had lost our first three games and in four and a half hours of football we hadn't managed to score. Tottenham scored after five minutes and we thought, 'here we go again'. Then Dwight Yorke equalised and we started to get our act together. It was close to the hour when we got a corner on the left and the ball came flying over. I got on the end of it and blasted it into the net. It was my first-ever goal for Villa and we were in the lead. It was a fantastic feeling. Tottenham later came back and won the game 3-2, but we had broken our duck and I was well-pleased with my goal.

"The supporters always want you to score plenty of goals but they also know when you are working hard for the team. When I went through a spell when the ball would just not go in the net they were brilliant, and they encouraged me every time I got the ball. They knew that I was trying hard and they responded to that.

"I have never compared myself to other strikers and I hope that no one else will do that either. Whether I am successful or not, I prefer that people think of me as Stan Collymore and not the Villa version of someone else."

One of his biggest fans is fellow Villa goal-getter, Dwight Yorke.

"Brian Little chased Stan for a long time and was prepared to pay top money for him because he knew, like the rest of us, that Stan is a quality player. His arrival at Villa Park was greeted with delight by the fans and the players alike. It put extra pressure on those of us who were also supposed to be scoring because it gave the manager greater options. There again, you expect that in top-class football and it is healthier for the club to have several scorers than just one or two. Stan is an outstanding player in that he not only scores great goals but that he also soaks up the pressure from opponents, leaving others with much more freedom to create and take scoring opportunities. I tell you, he is a quality player!"

Dwight Yorke is probably one of the most popular strikers of all time at Villa Park. He was discovered by the club while on tour in the West Indies. He was only 16 and still at school, but he was already an international for Trinidad and Tobago.

"The weather over here was a real shock to me. I was freezing all the time and I wore several lots of clothing while I was training. I think everyone thought I was crazy but I was so cold all the time.

"The other players and Graham Taylor were very encouraging though and they soon made me feel at home. I think that is why I always see Villa Park as my home now. I was a little fish in a big pool and I didn't really have a clue about professional football. I just played football for fun, but here it was a profession and totally different from what I had left behind me in the Caribbean.

"It took me a little while to get established in the side and then I had a bad injury problem which kept me out for a while and that was very frustrating. Things have got a lot better though and I have a few medals now.

"I love Aston Villa and I love the supporters. I also love living in the Midlands. There is always so much going on all the time and I have made many friends here. I hope I have scored a few goals that say thank you to everyone, and I hope I shall continue to say thank you many times in the future."

Like everyone else, strikers have their favourite moments and Dwight Yorke is no exception.

"I have had several favourite goals but I think that every striker wants to get a hat-trick in every game. One of my most memorable was a hat-trick against Newcastle a year or two ago. It was an amazing game at St James's Park and it was disappointing that we lost 4-3. However, it was a tremendous game in which to play and everyone who was there has since told me how fantastic it was to watch.

"One of my favourite goals was actually a penalty. We were drawing 0-0 with Sheffield United in the FA Cup. They were playing really well and we were having problems. When we were awarded a penalty I knew that it had to count because we might not get another opportunity like it. I thought that their goalkeeper, Alan Kelly, would decide to dive one way or the other, so I aimed for the middle of the goal and just to make sure I decided to chip it in case he stayed put. When I hit the ball he dived to the left and the ball sailed into the net like magic. The place went mad and everyone was talking about what a brilliant penalty it was. I had a look at it later in television and it did look pretty cool — so I enjoyed it all over again!"

When Dwight was trying to break into regular first-team football there were two other strikers keeping him out. Dalian Atkinson was one and Dean Saunders the other. Together they formed a lethal partnership.

"There's no doubt in my mind that Deano and I were made for each other," said Atkinson, who joined Villa from Real Sociedad in 1991. "He knew where to find me and I always knew where to find him. We developed an understanding almost from the first time we linked up. I thought Deano was just brilliant and he scored some fantastic goals which also inspired me to want to score great goals as well. We were good for each other!"

Dean Saunders, a huge signing from Liverpool in 1992, had been through a collection of clubs before joining Villa. Once he linked with Atkinson he looked happier and more confident than for some time.

"I joined Villa partly because things had not worked out at Liverpool, but also because I saw that Ron Atkinson was manager of a huge club with enormous ambition. I wanted to be a part of that. I had learned many lessons in my career up to becoming a Villa player and I wanted to prove that I was worth all the attention I had received, by helping Villa to win trophies."

He succeeded when Villa won the Coca-Cola Cup in 1994.

Guy Whittingham looked the part when he joined Villa in 1993. He was a fitness fanatic who had not been long out of the army. He had made a name for himself with Portsmouth and had been one of the top marksmen in the country when he signed for Villa.

"I did not even come into professional football until I was 24," said Guy. "If anyone had told me then that four years later I would be playing for a club as huge as Aston Villa, I would have laughed at them. It was an absolute dream."

It was also a dream for Cyrille Regis who first pulled on a Villa shirt when most players were thinking about retiring.

"I was 34 when I joined, and it gave me a real lift to be playing for Villa. I love the place and it was like starting my career all over again."

Regis proved to be a great help and inspiration to younger players like Dwight Yorke — and he scored a few goals along the way.

A recent addition to the list of Villa strikers was Savo

Milosevic. At times he has been brilliant while at other times he has been, not just frustrating, but downright annoying with an attitude problem that has been the bane of his managers' lives. Brian Little sat him down several times to try to help him get his act together.

"I had long chats with Savo, but I kept seeing myself in him when I was a player. I could understand his problems but doing something about them is not so easy as understanding. I still think he is an excellent player with all the potential to be one of the best strikers in the game."

Over the years Aston Villa have rarely suffered a shortage of goalscorers. With players like Lee Hendrie coming through it looks as if the opposition will continue to suffer at the hands of the Villa blitz for many years to come.

CHAPTER ELEVEN

THE LEADERS

WHAT is it like to be captain of Aston Villa? Few can say compared with the number of those who have pulled on the claret and blue shirt in the last fifty years or so. Everyone who has ever worn a Villa shirt will tell you what an honour it is to join the great list of talented footballers who have also proudly worn the shirt down through the years. One of the best known, Johnny Dixon, could not believe his ears when he was asked to be captain.

"I looked behind me because I thought the boss was talking to someone else. To this day I don't know why I was made captain. I should think that there were several other names ahead of mine on the list. I think I must have been the last resort when everyone else turned the job down! I never even dreamed that I would become a professional footballer, let alone play for Aston Villa, become captain and receive the FA Cup from the hands of Her Majesty the Queen. If I didn't have my medals and souvenirs I think I would wake up most mornings and think it was all a beautiful dream."

One of those souvenirs is his broken nose — but he didn't

collect that until the end of his career, the very end of his playing career in fact.

Johnny Dixon was born in County Durham in December 1923 and his early playing days were strictly amateur.

"I joined Spennymoor United when I was seventeen. Amateur football was very big in those days but it was very strictly amateur. Spennymoor was one of the best known clubs in the country and I was thrilled to be playing for them. When a Villa scout watched me and then asked if I might be interested in playing for them, I thought he must be joking. I knew I could play a bit, but Aston Villa was one of the biggest clubs in the country and it took a little while to sink in that I was of interest to them. I had a trial match and that was it.

"I decided to have a go and I played for Villa as an amateur at first. That was in 1944 when the war was still going on and there was no certain future for anyone. I played as an amateur until 1946 when I signed professional forms. It still took me a few years to become an established first-team player. I was gaining confidence all the time and I was enjoying being a professional. Of course we weren't paid a fortune in those days — I think I earned about £22 a week during the season and £20 during the summer as a retainer. We also received an extra £2 if we won, or £1 if we drew. I can't imagine what they earn today but, although it was not really a huge amount when I was playing, there were a lot of people earning a lot less than that so I don't think we had anything to complain about. There is a lot to be said for getting paid to do something which you would do for nothing."

The rest of Johnny Dixon's career is now a part of Villa folklore as he did indeed captain the side that won at Wembley — but he was also fearful of being remembered for something quite different.

"I'm sure it was an accident that I became captain in the first place. We had quite a few injuries and I was asked to step into the job temporarily and it just seemed to stick. I think we had a decent run so I was given the job permanently. My biggest worry was that in 1959 we were relegated and I really didn't like the idea of being remembered as the bloke who led Aston Villa down into the Second Division. I was very relieved when we won promotion the following season and regained our respect. It was a bit like scoring an own-goal. You desperately want to get one at the other end so that the memory of something going wrong is erased."

The broken nose?

"Oh yes, the broken nose. Would you believe it, it came during my very last competitive match. We were at home to Sheffield Wednesday in April 1961. It was our last game of the season and it was at Villa Park. I hadn't played in the first team all season and this was my retirement game. The club was in a comfortable position in the First Division, not in any danger and not in the running to win anything, so the manager, Joe Mercer, a lovely man, put me in the side so that I could say a proper goodbye to all the supporters. There were more than 26,000 in Villa Park and we beat Sheffield Wednesday 4-1. Gerry Hitchens scored a couple, Bobby Thomson got one and I scored as well. I was delighted with that, but then I got an accidental bash in the face and the last thing that the supporters saw of me was this old fellow walking off with a bloody nose. I didn't realise there and then that it was broken but it certainly gave me something to remember my final game by. Every time that I look in the mirror I see my souvenir!"

Johnny Dixon became youth coach at Villa Park for some years before he finally left and went into business as an ironmonger — later to retire. He is still going strong in his retirement and follows Villa avidly, going to games as often as he is able but mostly watching from the comfort of his armchair in front of the television.

Far from being remembered for any negative reasons, he is still held in extreme affection as the man who last lifted the FA Cup for Aston Villa.

Bruce Rioch was a very different kind of captain. While Johnny Dixon was an inspirational skipper who added an infectious sense of humour to his obvious playing skills, Bruce was the more studious type. He was a great player who captained Scotland. He had a very shrewd brain and he led by discipline and the sort of thinking capacity rarely seen today — and probably rarely seen in his day either.

"I fell in love with Aston Villa the moment I arrived at the ground," said Bruce. "I was already excited at the prospect of playing for the club but when I pulled on the shirt it was a very proud moment for me."

Rioch was born in Aldershot in September 1947, the third of four sons of Regimental Sergeant Major James Mackie Rioch of the Royal Scots Guards. His father was a keen athlete who represented Great Britain. He was also a strict disciplinarian who taught his sons the value of neatness, punctuality and directness.

"Being in the army meant that my father was used to dealing with men. Don't get me wrong, he brought us up with all the affection you could wish for and expect from a father, but he set certain standards that I am sure were of great benefit to us, especially later in life."

Bruce Rioch was also into athletics, but it had to take a back seat as his footballing talents became more and more obvious.

He joined Luton from school and made his League debut at the age of 16. His goalscoring ability made newspaper headlines and it was not long before he was being watched by several big clubs.

"Alec Stock was manager at Luton, a great boss and another disciplinarian. He called me after training one day and told me to get changed as we were going for a trip to meet officials of Aston Villa. 'They want to sign you and we are prepared to let you go at the right price', he told me. So off we went and I became a Villa player. My brother Neil soon followed, which was great for me having him around as we were good pals as well as brothers and he had also been at Luton."

The football world was a little shocked when the transfer took place because Villa had agreed a fee of £100,000, the first time that a six-figure amount had been paid for a player from the Third Division. Villa, however, knew that here was no ordinary player. He had already won a Fourth Division champions medal and, in that same season, he had scored 24 goals in 44 League matches — not bad for a twenty-year-old! It was July 1969 when Villa boss, Tommy Docherty, signed him and Rioch certainly had much to live up to. Within a year Villa had been relegated and he was suffering cartilage problems. Docherty had been sacked and to add insult to injury, as Villa went down Luton were promoted. Rioch, though, took it all in his stride.

"You have to be philosophical about these things. During my early years with Luton we were either in the promotion hunt or were fighting against relegation. I became conditioned to the extremes of football very quickly. Plenty of people said that I wasn't worth the money that Villa paid for me, especially since it was beginning to look as if I was injury prone. I don't think I really was, but that's how it must have seemed to some people. I think that a lot of the problem, if you can call it that, was the fact that Villa were not at the time in the First Division. If I had gone to one of the clubs in the top division for that sort of money, nobody would have said a thing. Since it was Villa in the Second Division, there was more than one angle to the transfer.

"It was a huge fee, I have never denied that, but I was both confident and determined to prove that it had been a good investment. The cartilage problems that I suffered during my early days with Villa seemed to confirm the suspicions of the cynics but it was almost a natural thing to happen. I had taken a lot of wear and tear on my legs for some years. I was playing first-team football earlier than most and so I got cartilage trouble earlier than most too. I had a few operations and I was then able to get on with my career."

Rioch's career at Villa saw him recover from his ailments and play a major part in the club's revival. He was a great tactician and was very quick-thinking, which made him a perfect feed for Andy Lochhead and the other strikers. He was also quite a scorer himself, but Bruce was always seen as a goal-creator rather than a scorer. A very practical person, it might come as a surprise to discover that he was in fact quite superstitious during his early playing days.

"I touched as much wood as possible before every game and I even used to hang a horseshoe on my peg for a while. I threw it away when it fell off one day and hit me on the head as I was bending down. I didn't think that was very lucky so the horseshoe was given the bullet!"

He made a major contribution to Villa's promotion from the Third Division, and captained the side which was developing into a squad capable of regaining First Division status.

"It was a great honour to be made captain. As I said before, I instantly fell in love with Aston Villa and that love has never diminished. I still feel the same for the club today. It was my ambition to see Villa back in the First Division and my only regret was that it came after I had left to join Derby in February 1974. I won a League championship medal with Derby but I would have loved to have had one from my Villa days.

"I don't know why I felt such an affinity with the club. It was just so impressive when I first went there. I could not believe that Villa were not in the top division fighting for the title. Villa Park was beautiful and the supporters were not only tremendous in their backing of the club but there were so many of them. They were totally dedicated and enthusiastic with Aston Villa in their blood. They haven't changed. They are still as great today and so is the club. It is wonderful to see Villa among the top clubs in the country and I have often wished that I was still a part of it."

Dennis Mortimer had the privilege of being captain of Aston Villa in the greatest hour of the club's history. He joined the club in December 1975 from Coventry, having already played more than 200 senior games for that team. In his ten years at Villa Park he added more than 400 games to that total and, by the time he retired, Dennis Mortimer had played well over 700 games for his various clubs.

Dennis became captain after the departure of Chris Nicholl. His appointment was the most casual affair that you could imagine.

"Ron Saunders was not the sort of man who went into long discussions about things. He made me captain simply by saying, 'Right, you lead 'em out!' That was it. No further instructions, no reasons why, no asking if I fancied the job. I was delighted of course. To be given such a great honour by someone like Ron Saunders was a huge compliment. It showed that he considered that I was mature enough to be able to handle it.

"As captain you have to lead by example on and off the pitch. It's not just a question of clapping your hands now and then and telling everyone else to keep going. You have to keep going yourself to inspire those around you, and off the pitch you have to be there to set a good example in conduct and professionalism. Other players have to be able to confide in you. It is not an easy task — but what a great privilege.

"I think the point that struck me most was that if we won something I would be the one who went up first to collect the trophy. That was a great prospect. Other than that my biggest job was to say the right word when the coin was tossed before the start of the game.

"The highlights of my career were collecting both the League championship and the European Cup. There is no doubt about that. On the one hand I could say that the European Cup was the greatest moment because so few captains have won it and, for Villa, it was the first and only time so far. However, Brian Clough once said that the greatest prize of all is the League championship, and I think I agree with him. When you look back over the last twenty years or so, there have not been that many clubs who have been champions. Several have won it a number of times but not many others have won it at all. Both occasions were very special and I am really grateful to have been in the right place at the right time to have earned such wonderful honours."

Dennis Mortimer was also captain when Villa won the European Super Cup and travelled to Tokyo for the World Club championship against Penarol. His Villa matches and England 'B', Under-23 and youth commitments, made him a much travelled man. Today he is heavily involved with the Professional Footballers Association's coaching programmes, but still finds time to follow the fortunes of Aston Villa.

"They were not only my club but you cannot go through what we went through together without forming a real attachment. It had been 71 years between League championships when we last won the title. I hope it will not be too long before another Villa captain wins the Premiership."

A few years after Dennis Mortimer had moved on, David Platt became captain. He had already been skipper of Crewe and Graham Taylor decided to make him leader of Villa too.

"He was used to responsibility and he also had the right attitude," said Taylor. "You only had to look at his career up to that point to see that he was a fighter and would never just give in. You need that sort of inspiration from your captain and you also need someone with a brain. There is no question over David Platt's brain. He is an intelligent fellow and he has done very well for himself. I never had any hesitation in making him captain at Villa and also for England."

For Platt, the moment he was made captain came as a pleasant surprise.

"I have always been the sort of person who likes to be in front, taking the lead, but I never expected that one day I would be skipper at such a great club as Aston Villa. I was almost speechless when I was asked. It was a great honour. The Villa have had a great tradition of excellent captains over the years, and to be added to such a list was a very great honour. It is difficult to put into words but it gives you such a tremendous ride to lead the side out."

Kevin Richardson was another popular captain, signed by Ron Atkinson from Real Sociedad in 1991, but previously a winner with Arsenal.

"Kevin was a player's player," said Big Ron. "I bought him to work hard and make life difficult for the opposition. I had seen plenty of Kevin when he was playing for other people and I knew that he was the sort of player I wanted in our side. I knew the other players would respect him and would be motivated by him, so I knew he would make a good captain."

It worked. A few years later he captained the Villa side that won the Coca-Cola Cup at Wembley.

"I had spoken to Dalian Atkinson before I agreed to join Villa. He had worked for Ron Atkinson before and spoke very highly about him. That was good enough for me. Other clubs were interested in me but Ron just got on with making the arrangements while everyone else was still talking about it. That impressed me and I then really wanted to be a part of his Villa set-up. Becoming captain was a big bonus, especially when we played at Wembley in the Coca-Cola Cup Final."

Andy Townsend also proved to be a popular captain. He was another of Ron Atkinson's choices.

"The club had not had a player like Andy since David Platt left. He was strong, progressive, had energy and ability, and I knew that he would give us the bit of drive that we were missing from midfield before he arrived. Andy always took care of himself so I knew he would be good for four or five seasons even though he was just turning thirty. He was one of those durable players who could go on for as long as they wanted. I also knew he would make a good captain and I think he proved that himself."

"I was smitten from the moment that I walked into Villa

Park," said Townsend. "You see places differently when you are an opposition player, but now I was a Villa player and I could appreciate the place properly. Everything about Aston Villa is fabulous. You could feel it the moment that you walked into the place. Everything is brilliantly organised from top to bottom and yet it retains that nice casual atmosphere.

"I found it very flattering to be asked to be captain of Aston Villa, but I knew it was what I wanted to be. There is so much history in the club that you desperately want to become a part of it. There were quite a few young players there at the time and I made sure that I helped them as much as possible while not neglecting the older players who had all the experience but still needed encouragement. Being captain of Villa was one of the best times of my career."

As well as being a real leader on the pitch, Andy Townsend also provided some entertaining moments off the pitch as he had a reputation as a practical joker — and also as a guitarist.

"I like my music. I play a bit of guitar but I have never played in a band. I get enough stick playing football without subjecting myself to even more as a musician. Playing the guitar is just a way for me to relax although I have become a bit of an addict. I see the guitar leaning against the wall and it just sort of says, 'Come and pick me up'. Do you know what I mean?

Yes Andy, of course we do!

More recently, Gareth Southgate has been charged with the job of leading the Villa pack. His task of inspiring others could have been made all the more difficult by his legendary penalty miss in Euro '96 — but not at Villa.

"The mickey-taking still goes on," said Ugo Ehiogu. "He knows it ain't ever going to stop. But he's big enough to take it, and it wouldn't be any different at any other club. In truth, everyone admires, respects, and thinks a lot of him and reckon he's a pretty good bloke to have as skipper."

Southgate had captained Crystal Palace to the First Division championship in 1994 before Villa signed him, and Brian Little knew he was on a safe bet if he made him captain after the departure of Andy Townsend.

"We needed good character and spirit on the field and even more commitment, and I knew that Gareth could supply all of that. Gareth is the sort of player that every manager would like in their side. I knew he would make a good captain because he had already done that elsewhere under difficult circumstances. He was popular with the other players and the supporters but he took his responsibilities seriously, and I knew that Aston Villa mattered to him."

There were immediate comparisons with David Platt and Gareth felt quite flattered by that.

"If I can do half as well as David and go on to be successful with Aston Villa and then become captain of England, it would be magnificent. Not only is it an honour to be compared with David but it is also an immense privilege to captain Villa. My ambition really is to be the next captain to lift the Premiership trophy."

And that's a thought we all share.

CHAPTER TWELVE

THE LEAGUE CUP

THE League Cup has been won by 21 clubs since it was started in 1961 but, no matter how any of the clubs go on to success in this competition, Villa have one record that can never be beaten — they were the very first! In its early days, not all League clubs entered the competition and the Final was held on a two-leg basis rather than being a Wembley showpiece. Nothing of that detracts from the fact that it was still a tough competition which needed special effort to be won. There is no doubt that there is glory eternal in being in the history books as the inaugural victors of the League Cup.

Villa's very first game in the League Cup was on 12 October 1960, when 17,057 fans turned up at Villa Park to see the visit of Huddersfield as the overture for what was to climax in a grand finale nearly a year later. Ron Wylie was in the side and scored twice as Villa knocked out Huddersfield with a 4-1 win.

"I don't think we knew what to make of it at that stage. We knew that it was a new competition of course, but it was early days and there were a lot of critics who said that there was already more than enough football and that it was pointless to add yet another meaningless competition. As it happens, the League Cup became quite an important competition over the following years. To us at the time it was just another game when we took on Huddersfield but, after we had won that one and then beat Preston in the next round, we started to enjoy ourselves. By the time we had beaten Plymouth and Wrexham to reach the semi-final we had begun to take the competition very seriously."

The semi-final went to three games because Burnley proved to be tough opponents. After drawn games at both Villa Park and Turf Moor, the two teams met again at Old Trafford where Villa won 2-1 thanks to a Stan Lynn penalty and a winner from Gerry Hitchens. The Final itself was not played until early the following season — a fact which did little to enhance the esteem of the competition. Rotherham were the other Finalists and Alan Deakin was in the side for both legs of the tie.

"I don't think we were quite ready for what happened in the first leg at Millmoor. We were the favourites as you would expect because we were in the higher division, but we did not approach the game with any degree of over-confidence. The League season had only just started three days earlier and we had lost our opening game 2-0 at Everton, so we were not in the mood to let Rotherham do the same thing to us. They did though! They played extremely well and they gave us a really hard time. We trooped off at the end hardly able to believe that we had been beaten 2-0 yet again.

"There were a few words spoken and then we had three League matches before the return leg at Villa Park. We didn't lose any of those three games, in fact we won two and drew at Wolves, so by the time Rotherham arrived for the second leg we were more than ready to try and pull back that two-goal deficit. We had the better of the opening phase of the game but the rain was pouring down and we were kicking against the wind. We just could not get our act together properly and by half-time it was still 0-0. We were told to keep calm and keep playing football and it would all fall into place, so that's what we did and gradually were able to take control of the game. I put a pass through to Alan O'Neill and he stuck the ball into the bottom corner of the net. Soon after that, Harry Burrows got a shooting chance and he used to send them in like thunderbolts. Sure enough, he let fly and the ball smacked into the back of the net to make it 2-2. We had left it a bit late and the game went into extra-time. Rotherham gave us a scare or two before the end of the ninety minutes but, when extra-time began, I think that it's fair to say there was only going to be one winner.

"Peter McParland scored a third and that was it. Looking back now I am proud of having won that tankard but I wish it had been at Wembley. I suppose there are those that say that the competition was devalued by certain teams not taking part, but those games still had to be won and, as far as I am concerned, I believe that Aston Villa can be justifiably proud in being the first name on the list of League Cup winners."

That was, of course, just the start of the League Cup and Villa's successes in a competition that grew in status but appears to have declined a little in recent years. To those who reach the Final it is a great achievement, but among the bigger clubs the lure of Europe has become much more important. I wonder how many managers have secretly wished they had taken the League Cup more seriously when their dreams of glory in other competitions have faded.

Villa reached the League Cup Final in 1963 when, once

again, it was held on a two-leg basis. To add to the excitement, Birmingham City were the opponents. Bobby Thomson scored in the first leg at St Andrew's, but the Blues scored three of their own and that was the advantage that they took to Villa Park for the tense second leg. George Graham — later to enjoy great success with Arsenal — played in both legs.

"I had only just made my debut for Villa, less than a week before the first leg. I was raw, of course, but I was enthusiastic. I played in the League match at home to Liverpool and scored as we beat them 2-0. It gave me a tremendous boost. Three days later I was in the side that drew 1-1 at Ipswich in our last League match of the season. Two days later was the League Cup Final first leg, so it was all a bit hectic.

"We were very disappointed to lose 3-1 and we were determined to do better in the second leg four days later. Birmingham were equally determined though, and they were in the driving seat. All they had to do was to stop us and the trophy was theirs. They did it very effectively and the match ended at 0-0 which gave them an aggregate 3-1 win.

"I was unhappy like the rest of the side. In the space of nine days I had gone from walking on clouds to being totally fed-up. Still, that's football and especially that's Cup football!"

In the years that followed the League Cup grew in status but Villa rarely strayed beyond the opening rounds. In the 1966-67 season there was a further embarrassment when West Bromwich knocked Villa out of the competition with a 6-1 hiding — another local derby result that needed retribution. The chance came three years later, but West Bromwich did it again, this time with a 2-1 win at Villa Park which sent the club tumbling out of the competition yet again.

The 1970-71 season saw Villa reach their third League Cup

Final and this time the match was to be a one-off game at Wembley. Tottenham were favourite since they were a First Division side while Villa were still in Division Three. Some say that the League Cup run actually cost Villa promotion, but who can really say that the club would have finished any higher than fourth anyway?

On the way to Wembley, Villa had amazed everyone by beating Manchester United in the two-leg semi-final. Andy Lochhead was in both games and scored in both too.

"The first leg at Old Trafford was like a Cup Final to us. We fancied our chances but United were a formidable outfit. When you face players like Best, Charlton, Law, Crerand and the others, you know that you're in for a hard time. Nobody expected us to get a result but we came away with a 1-1 draw and we were delighted about that.

"I think there were nearly 60,000 in Villa Park for the second leg, but I believe that the tickets could have been sold several times over. United piled on the pressure right from the start and we really had to defend in strength. Brian Kidd scored for them with a spectacular scissor-kick, but we went level after half-time because I managed to get one for us. The atmosphere was fantastic and the game was swinging backwards and forwards. We had just under twenty minutes left when Pat McMahon scored with a beautiful header. The place went mad. United threw everything at us then but we stood firm and won 3-2 on aggregate.

"By comparison the Final at Wembley was a bit of an anti-climax. It was great to be at Wembley but we never really got going properly and Martin Chivers scored twice to give Tottenham their 2-0 victory. It was a long trip home from Wembley and we felt desperately sorry for the supporters who had been brilliant throughout the League Cup campaign."

Four years later Villa were back at Wembley for another League Cup Final. On the way they had overcome Everton with a 3-0 win at Goodison Park. After that, victories over Crewe, Hartlepool, Colchester and Chester gave Villa a date with Norwich. Ray Graydon proved to be Villa's hero on the day.

"There was a fantastic atmosphere at Wembley. Whether you are playing in the FA Cup or the League Cup it is a time you will always remember. You soak up as much as you can because you know that it might never happen to you again.

"The first half was not that good. It was 0-0 and there was a bit of a deadlock. The goalkeepers didn't have that much to do. In the dressing-room at half-time we did a bit of refocussing and when we restarted we gave Norwich a tough time. Kevin Keelan was in the Norwich goal and he was really busy — to his credit, he was brilliant. Jim Cumbes was in our goal and he was getting a bit cold while Kevin Keelan was definitely keeping warm.

"We still couldn't score though — until ten minutes before the end. Chris Nicholl flew in to meet Chico Hamilton's corner and sent in a great header. It was a goal all the way but Mel Machin stopped it with his hands and we had a penalty. I tried to forget all about where I was and how important that penalty was as I stepped up to take it. I blasted the shot and couldn't believe it when Keelan pushed it away. The ball hit the post and rebounded to my feet. I didn't pass up that second chance and we went ahead."

It proved to be the only goal of the match and, with all due respect to Norwich, the second half had been all Villa's and justice was served.

Andy Gray also has a particular memory of the League Cup and Aston Villa.

"My very first home game for Villa was in the League Cup. I had only just signed from Dundee United and of course I wanted to make a good impression with the supporters as well as with my team-mates and the manager. I had made my club debut in a 0-0 draw away to Middlesbrough four days earlier, but now I was going to come under the scrutiny of the fans at Villa Park. What a game it promised to be — against Manchester United in the League Cup. As holders of the trophy, Villa wanted to keep a grip on it — but United were equally hungry for success, whatever the competition.

"The atmosphere at Villa Park was fantastic. The only times I had played in front of really big crowds at Dundee United were when we played against Celtic or Rangers. Now here I was, making my home debut with more than 40,000 people watching me. The air was electric throughout the game and I am not proud of the fact that we lost the game 2-1. There was some consolation for me however — I scored our goal and I was given a great reception by the fans. That was not just my home club debut but also my debut in the competition. It ended in defeat but with the hope of better things to come.

The following season Villa were in the League Cup Final again, this time at Wembley in March 1977. Once again there was both delight and despair for Andy Gray.

"I played in every round of the competition. We beat Manchester City, then Norwich, Wrexham and Millwall to get to the semi-final, and then we had a hard slog against Queen's Park Rangers. It took three games before the tie was settled and we had booked our place in the Final against Everton. It was a great experience to be playing at Wembley and we had quite a game in front of nearly 100,000 supporters and the television cameras. It was a deadlock though at 0-0 and we had to play again. Four days later we replayed the Final at Hillsborough in front of nearly 55,000. This time we finished at 1-1 after extra-time and a third game was arranged for Old Trafford a month later.

"I took a knock in between the games and injured my ankle ligaments, which meant that I could not play in the rearranged Final. However, I watched the game and I was as thrilled as anyone when we won 3-2. It was a hard game to play in but it was even harder to watch. Everton took the lead and held it until eight minutes from the end when Chris Nicholl let fly with a left-foot shot and the ball smashed into the net for the equaliser. A minute later we went ahead when Brian Little scored. Everton went straight back to the other end and Mike Lyons equalised for them. The place was in uproar but there were no more goals and once again extra-time was needed. The deadlock was finally broken for the last time, almost at the end of extra-time, when Brian Little suddenly found himself in possession. Everyone was tired out and I think Brian only just had the energy to slip the ball over the line from just a few yards out. It was a great result for Villa and I was as delighted as anyone, even though my pleasure was spoiled a little by the disappointment of being unable to take part in that final game. I managed to limp around the pitch with the lads for a lap of honour. A Villa fan on the touchline handed me a huge top hat and I wore it all the way round Old Trafford. It was some consolation for not being able to play and part of the lesson you learn in this great game is — never take anything for granted."

Gary Shaw also has fond memories of the League Cup.

"I scored my first senior goals for Villa in the League Cup. It was in August 1979. I had my first-team debut the previous season but I hadn't scored. We began the League Cup campaign a couple of weeks after the start of the new season and we were drawn against Colchester in the second round. We had to play them away first and then play a return at Villa Park a week later. I can remember scoring both our goals in the 2-0 away win. I can even remember that the first was a header and the second was a volley. You don't forget things like that. Those were my first goals and I think they gave me a lot of confidence because I finished the season as Villa's top League scorer."

That drawn out affair with Everton was Villa's last League Cup Final for seventeen years. Between those years, though, there was in the 1981-82 campaign, a golden opportunity to assert themselves over West Bromwich. Wolves had already been beaten in the second round but West Bromwich proved to be a jinx team once again as they beat Villa 1-0 in the fifth round. Two years later however, revenge was gained when Villa beat the Albion 2-1 at the Hawthorns in the fourth round of the competition. There was a repeat performance in the fourth round two years later. The 1988-89 season also saw some fun for Villa as they were drawn out of the hat with Birmingham City in the two-leg second round. The first game at St Andrew's ended with a 2-0 scoreline in Villa's favour, and in the return Villa ran riot to win 5-0 on the night and thus 7-0 on aggregate.

The 1993-94 season proved to be the next big one for Villa. It all began at St Andrew's where Kevin Richardson scored the only goal of the match in the first leg of the second round. Dean Saunders scored in the return at Villa Park and a round three trip to Sunderland was next in line. Villa won a convincing 4-1 victory at Roker Park only to be rewarded with a trip to Highbury for the fourth round. When Dalian Atkinson grabbed the winner, Villa justifiably began thinking about Wembley. The fifth round meant yet another trip to North London — this time to Tottenham. Ray Houghton and Earl Barrett scored

Villa's goals in the 2-1 victory and now only Tranmere stood between Aston Villa and Wembley.

The semi-final clash between the two clubs was a classic. Dalian Atkinson kept Villa's hopes alive in the first leg at Prenton Park when he scored in injury time. Tranmere were 3-0 ahead at the time. The return leg was a tremendously exciting game. Once again it was Dalian Atkinson to the rescue. Injury time was imminent and the scoreline was 2-1 in Villa's favour. Another goal was needed and Dalian produced it in the last minute. Extra-time failed to change the score and the game went to penalties. Enter another hero — Mark Bosnich! Bossie saved three penalties and Villa were off to Wembley to meet Manchester United who were chasing an unprecedented treble of championship, FA Cup and League Cup. Ultimately, United did win the double but a great performance by Villa denied them another piece of history. Dalian Atkinson scored in the first half, Dean Saunders added a second before Mark Hughes pulled one back — and then, two minutes from the end, Saunders scored from the penalty spot after a Kanchelskis hand-ball.

Kevin Richardson had the captain's privilege of collecting the trophy.

"Lifting the Cup as captain and being named 'Man of the Match' was a great honour for me. Everybody played their part and we came out on top. We were under a lot more pressure than we had anticipated but we took our chances and we took them well!"

Manager, Ron Atkinson, was thrilled.

"We always felt that we were fated to win as all our best performances had been in the Coca-Cola Cup. We had the belief that the Cup was going to be ours. I was delighted by the way we played in the Final. We played against the best team in the country and matched them in every department."

Two-goal Dean Saunders also revelled in the success.

"I don't think anyone fancied us to win but we really got our act together. When the boss named five men in midfield we thought it would either be a great success or a complete disaster — it turned out to be a success!"

Tony Daley was perhaps a little more realistic.

"To be honest, we were a bit tired at half-time — but we went out, took a lot of pressure, and then took our chances. I thought we played very well and always looked likely to take control. There were dangers that they might have got the upper hand but, in the end, we deserved to win!"

In 1996 Villa's name was once again etched on the Coca-Cola Cup. A 7-1 win over Peterborough was the result of the two-leg second round tie. Stockport, Queen's Park Rangers and Wolves were all toppled before the semi-final in which Arsenal provided the opposition. Two Dwight Yorke goals at Highbury sealed the tie and the club was heading for Wembley yet again. Leeds were in the opposing corner.

The result of the 1996 Coca-Cola Cup Final was probably the penultimate nail in the coffin of Howard Wilkinson's career as manager of Leeds United. Dwight Yorke, who had missed the 1994 Final, was on a personal mission.

"One of my own ambitions was to play at Wembley and it had been a great disappointment to me when I missed the League Cup Final against Manchester United in 1994. The 1996 Final gave me the chance to make up for that disappointment."

He certainly did too. Dwight and his team-mates played out of their skins to humiliate Leeds and win 3-0. It could have been many more. Savo Milosevic opened the scoring in the first half, Ian Taylor made it two and Dwight Yorke scored the much-deserved third. Andy Townsend collected the trophy.

"It was a brilliant day. The Leeds supporters were shell-shocked while our own were having a party. I don't think that Leeds played as badly as everyone said. We were on form and I think we would have beaten just about anybody on that day. It was a great experience and one I shall always remember."

For Mark Draper it was also a day to remember.

"That was definitely my best day in football so far. We all have our ups and downs and beating Leeds at Wembley that day made up for all my downs. I was surprised by how relaxed I felt. It was such a big game but everyone was absolutely calm. When we got to within a couple of miles of Wembley we could see all the supporters and that's when the old adrenalin started going. Walking out in that wonderful stadium was the next great experience and then, of course, came the celebrations which started directly the final whistle blew. You can never forget a day like that!"

Career highlights are born from competitions like the League Cup. Nobody has won the competition more times than Aston Villa. Only Liverpool have won as many. Every victory has seen the streets of Birmingham lined with cheering supporters. Every victory has been the climax of a trail of talent and toil. Don't tell those who have won it that the League Cup is a second-rate competition because they have the scars and the trophies to prove you wrong.

Brian Little has been both Villa player and manager of successful Villa sides and knows what he is talking about when he says, "Call it whatever you want, but the League Cup is a unique competition. All 92 clubs start out — but only one finishes. That's what makes it unique to whoever lifts the trophy!"

CHAPTER THIRTEEN

THE MAGIC OF THE FA CUP

T HERE is nothing quite like it! The FA Cup is famous throughout the world. For decades it was reported on extensively by the various media all over the globe. Then came television, and now the game itself is shown live to hundreds of millions of viewers on every continent. Hundreds of millions more receive the recorded highlights.

Aston Villa are one of the undisputed Kings of the FA Cup with no fewer than seven victories out of nine appearances in the Final. There were three famous triumphs last century, two more before World War One, another between wars, and then the Wembley success in 1957 — one of the most controversial in the history of the competition.

Why controversial?

When a forward from one side collides with a goalkeeper from another side, resulting in the loss of that goalkeeper — that's controversy! Today the incident would be shown again and again from every possible angle with computer technology that can prove any side of any argument. In 1957, these techniques were still in the embryonic stage and we have to rely on the eye-witness accounts of those who were there.

The run-up to that Final, which was Villa's first since 1924, was as exciting as the Final itself. It was the 1956-57 season and steadily Villa had made their way through the rounds, although their progress was far from plain sailing. They needed a replay to master Luton in the third round, had a battle royal to win 3-2 at Middlesbrough in the fourth round, had to work hard for a 2-1 home win over Bristol City in the next round, and then beat Burnley after a replay in the sixth round.

The semi-final had extra spice because it was a derby tie against West Bromwich Albion on the neutral ground of Molineux.

"Before the draw for the semi-final was made, we were looking at the possibility of an all-Midlands Final," said Johnny Dixon. "Birmingham City were also in the last four and only Manchester United were non-Midlands. We knew that West Brom would be our toughest opponents yet but we were well prepared for it.

"I think on the day that they might have just been the better footballing side, but we were the more determined and even though they were winning 2-1 with just five minutes to go we would not give up. Some of us had seen what could happen in the dying minutes and we threw everything into getting an equaliser. Billy Myerscough got the ball out on the right and swung it into their box. Peter McParland rose up like a swan out of the water and headed it home. It was a wonderful goal and earned us a replay. Peter had scored our previous goal after Albion had gone ahead after about two minutes."

There were 55,000 fans in Molineux for that Saturday

afternoon game and the following Thursday another 58,000 piled into St Andrew's for the replay.

"It was another exciting game. West Bromwich lost Ronnie Allen about halfway through the first half with an injury — and I think that ruined their plans. Ronnie was hurt in a collision with Jimmy Dugdale who had won the FA Cup as an Albion player in 1954. They were old team-mates and Jimmy would not have deliberately set out to hurt him. The supporters gave him some stick though for the rest of the game. About seven minutes before half-time, Peter McParland put a cross over which looked as if it was going into the goalkeeper's arms — but Billy Myerscough popped up again and dived headlong at the ball. Next thing we knew it was in the back of the net and we were ahead. The score stayed at 1-0 although we both had chances to score more. West Brom had the best chance when they had an open goal and the ball just rolled against the post instead of going in. I should think they gave up at that stage.

"Going to Wembley was a wonderful experience. I don't think I have ever seen so many people in one place. The atmosphere was fantastic.

"In the dressing-room before the game we were all a bit nervous and we helped settle ourselves by opening telegrams and letters from fans wishing us all the best. It seemed like the time was dragging and then, all of a sudden, we were walking out into the stadium with Eric Houghton leading us alongside Manchester United led by Matt Busby.

"The Duke of Edinburgh came down to meet the teams and, as captain, I had the privilege of introducing him to everyone. He took an interest and had a comment or two for everyone. He seemed to know something about us all. Then Roger Byrne, the United captain, and I went to the centre for the toss and suddenly the game was under way and the controversy was about to begin.

Peter McParland was the forward at the centre of the controversy and he vividly recalls the day and the moment.

"Les Smith put the ball over from the right. You get a feeling about these things and I just knew that the ball was destined for the back of the net. You don't get much time for thinking, but I was going to aim to put it into the far corner of the net. Everything was right and I should have scored. Somehow though I didn't get my aim right and I headed it straight into Ray Wood's arms as he raced towards me. I was racing in as he was racing out. and we were on an inevitable collision course. In those days you could go in on a goalkeeper because, if he dropped the ball, you had as much right to it as he did. You could even charge the goalkeeper, shoulder to shoulder, so there was no reason for me to stop dead. Woody kept coming and he *did* have a reputation for being a brave guy. We would have met shoulder to shoulder if he had not pulled out at the last minute. However, instead of meeting with our shoulders, his jaw hit the side of my face and he had to go off with a fractured cheekbone.

"There were those who thought that I had deliberately tried to hurt him, and there were others who said that I laughed as Woody lay on the ground. Both suggestions were wrong and extremely hurtful. My thoughts were with him as he was being stretchered off. I wouldn't have wished that on anyone — especially in such a unique match as the FA Cup Final. As for laughing, nobody seemed to realise that I had also been hurt and had quite a lump on the side of my face. I was moving my jaw about to check it out and obviously it looked to some that I was laughing — but I most definitely was not!"

The Manchester United fans were far from happy. The

referee dealt with the incident as an accident but they felt that he should have taken some disciplinary action.

"If the same thing happened today the referee would probably show me a yellow card — but the rules were different then and I had done nothing wrong. I was booed throughout the rest of that first half and it was a far from pleasant experience. You always want your memories of playing in an FA Cup Final at Wembley to be happy ones. This one was far from happy for me. By half-time I was feeling really depressed until Bill Moore, out trainer, came to my rescue. He said, 'Right, they're booing you and the only way to shut them up is to get out there and stick one in their net!' Bill gave me back my attitude and I felt much better by the time we started the second half."

Villa took control in that second half and, as more and more chances were created, it was obvious that the game was not going to end with a blank score-sheet.

"Johnny Dixon hit a beautiful cross from the right and I met it with my head. It went in like a bullet. I had already hit the post with a similar effort a little earlier and so to see this one go in gave me a marvellous feeling."

That was in the 68th minute. Manchester United's shoulders sagged. Jackie Blanchflower had taken over in goal and had done extremely well — but there was no stopping that goal. Five minutes later the destination of the trophy was sealed.

"Johnny Dixon sent in a shot which smacked against the bar and rebounded. Billy Myerscough and I both went for it, but I got there first and volleyed it into the net."

The game was by no means over. Ray Wood had returned to the match on the wing just for nuisance value. When Manchester United pulled a goal back with six minutes to go —

Tommy Taylor heading home a Duncan Edwards corner — the scene was set for a frantic finale. Wood went back in goal and Villa found themselves under siege. However, Villa's defence was not breached and, when the final whistle went, Villa arms were raised aloft while United knees sank to the ground.

The controversy? To this date, McParland maintains that it was a fair challenge within the rules of the day. Wood was not so sure but the two of them shook hands in a genuine show of friendship immediately after the game. Bobby Charlton — at nineteen, a surprise member of the United team for the Final — described the incident as "an unfortunate clashing of heads", but perhaps the final word should be an independent one.

Frank Coultas was referee on that day and has been asked many times about the affair.

"Personally I saw nothing vicious in the charge. It was clumsy but there was no foul intent. I gave the foul because Wood went down, otherwise I would have allowed play to continue. I felt sorry for Wood because of his injury, but I also felt sorry for McParland because I'm sure he had no intention of hurting his opponent."

The controversy continued after the game and it was far from over for McParland.

"Some of the press reports the next day made it seem as if I had deliberately put Woody out of the game. It was totally untrue. Then the abusive letters began and, in many ways, I have had to live with that ever since. I know it was an accident and everyone else who was nearby knew it was an accident. In today's game I would have been shown a yellow card and United would have been allowed to bring on a substitute goalkeeper, but the game was different then. Nothing that happened was illegal or done to gain an unfair advantage. Fortunately I still have the memory of scoring our two goals and receiving a winner's medal from Her Majesty the Queen."

Aston Villa have not appeared in the FA Cup Final since 1957, but there are many among today's fans who were there on the day or, at the very least, saw the game on television. They have had their moments since, but the Twin Towers have eluded them in this competition. In the 1960s they rarely went beyond the fifth round, but there were some exciting clashes in the earlier rounds — especially when they met old rivals, Wolves, who twice dumped them out of the competition at crucial stages.

Commercial activities were not like they are today, and it was quite a novelty to see the Villa squad endorsing 'Wolsey X Briefs and Vests' — available at stockists throughout the country and made from a finely knit cotton fibre full of natural elasticity.

Money was on the menu for some at Wembley though, as ticket touts devoured whatever they could obtain and then spat them out again to the desperate fans — always at mega-prices. For instance, 50 shilling tickets (£2.50) were on sale for nine pounds, while tickets at three shillings and sixpence (17½p) were inflated to three pounds, ten shillings (£3.50).

Food of a different sort came in the shape of 8,000 sandwiches, 5,000 pies and countless packets of crisps with salt wrapped in little twists of blue paper. Perhaps the most endearing form of catering was the chewing gum which Villa players favoured for use throughout the game. They were so excited by their victory that they completely forgot to remove it before collecting the trophy and their medals from Her Majesty the Queen. Johnny Dixon was mortified.

"Do you mean to say that millions of TV viewers saw me

chewing gum as the Queen handed me the Cup? Oh no! Oh no!"

Not all the memories of classic FA Cup encounters are of victories however. Take January of 1948 for instance, when 65,000 fans crammed into Villa Park for the third-round tie between Villa and Manchester United. Sailor Brown was in the Villa side.

"It was a very wet day and we knew that it was not the sort of day to make mistakes. It was slippery in places and the ball would skid, while in other places it would get bogged down — so really anything could happen! It was a crunch game because both United and ourselves were among the hot favourites to reach the Final.

"We kicked-off and had the ball in the net straight away. Trevor Ford took the kick-off, passed it to me and I slipped a couple of players before passing to Leslie Smith. He cut in from the wing, passed to George Edwards and George let fly. None of their players had touched the ball and the goal was timed at thirteen and a half seconds!

"The place was in uproar but, rather than take the wind out of United's sails, it seemed to actually encourage them to greater effort because they came at us like a team possessed. We might as well have gone home at that point because they played as if we were not there. Within six minutes Jack Rowley had equalised from a corner. Just ten minutes later they got another corner and Morris put them in the lead. They seemed to step up another gear after that. We did have our moments but it was like swimming against the tide. They got another goal after half an hour. Rowley took a free-kick and it hit one of our defenders and went straight to Pearson. He said, 'Thank you very much' and put it straight into the net. Morris headed another a few minutes later and then Delaney made it 5-1 just before half-time.

"You can imagine what it was like in our dressing-room. We were all a bit shell-shocked to say the least and if someone had suggested not bothering to go out for the second half we would have been delighted. At times like that you need a good manager — and we had Alex Massie. Instead of having a moan about the first half, he said, 'Keep your chins up lads. They've had the run of the ball. Your task is not impossible. Just go out there and do your best for the next forty-five minutes, that's all I ask.'

"Well that really did give us a lift. We had gone in nursing aching limbs and aching hearts, but now we couldn't wait to get out for the second half. Within minutes I got us a corner. George Edwards took it and put such a swerve on the ball that it went straight into the net. Our tails were up now and the crowd got behind us. Trevor Ford had the ball in the net but it was disallowed. The game became a bit cut and thrust after that but we were getting the best of it. There were about twenty minutes left when Dickie Dorsett had a terrific shot from a free-kick. He could really hit a ball could Dickie. His shot was deflected but Les Smith got the rebound and made it 5-3.

"The crowd was really going mad by now and we were carried along by the noise. With ten minutes left Trevor Ford looked certain to get another goal when he was brought down. The referee pointed straight to the spot and Dickie Dorsett didn't hesitate in taking it. Sooner him than me because the penalty area was a real mud bath by this time. No problem for Dickie though. He fired the ball straight in and it was 5-4.

"Trevor Ford hit the bar just after that and then United broke away and got a corner. Pearson put his foot to the cross and in it went. United were 6-4 ahead. That was it! No more goals. A little while later the referee blew his whistle to end it and we all shook hands. When I looked up there were 65,000 people applauding us off and I think it was then that I realised that I had just taken part in a 'classic' Cup-tie."

A couple of years before the United game, there had been another Cup-tie to remember when Villa faced Derby County in March 1946. The attendance for the home leg of that FA Cup sixth-round tie was 76,588 — a record that still stands half a century later and probably for ever. Goalkeeper Alan Wakeman remembers the game vividly.

"We had enjoyed our Cup run. They were all played over two legs in those post-war days, until you got to the semi-finals. We had beaten Coventry in the third round and then knocked out Millwall with an aggregate of 13-3, which included a 9-1 win at home. Then we beat Chelsea and were drawn against Derby.

"It was a massive crowd. We were used to big crowds, but this one was huge. We didn't know at the time that it was a Villa Park record, and we certainly didn't expect it to be the biggest of all time at the ground.

"It was an exciting game for the fans, end-to-end stuff in which I think it's fair to say we had the edge. George Edwards, Bob Iverson and Frank Broome had each scored a goal for us while Derby had scored two. With five minutes left it was 3-2 and then the Raich Carter-Peter Doherty partnership went into top gear for Derby and they scored two late goals to end with a 4-3 scoreline.

"In the second leg we took the initiative again, but it ended in a 1-1 draw and we were out. But it was a very exciting tie, especially the first leg, and for years people said that it was the most thrilling Cup-tie they had ever seen. Perhaps it still is."

In 1954-55 there was another epic tie — this time against Doncaster Rovers. It was not that there was a goal spree but that a series of drawn games had to be replayed. It was the fourth round of the FA Cup and the first meeting was a 0-0 draw at Doncaster. The replay at Villa Park ended at 2-2, so they met again — this time at neutral Maine Road. That result was 1-1 and another replay was necessary. Hillsborough was the venue and 0-0 the result, with bad light preventing extra-time because of the lack of floodlighting. Finally a fourth replay was arranged for the Hawthorns — and this time Doncaster won 3-1.

Johnny Dixon, who was later to taste FA Cup success with Villa, said after the fourth replay. "We were sick of the sight of them. On paper we should have seen them off in the first game. We were among the leaders in the First Division and they were fighting relegation from the Second. However, football is not as predictable as that — otherwise people would be winning jackpots every week. We huffed and we puffed but they still kept coming back for more."

The 1970s followed a similar pattern with very little to put into the history books. The decade started with two very incon-spicuous results. The 1970-71 season saw Villa beaten in the first round by Torquay of the Third Division. Southend knocked out Villa 1-0, also in the first round. Admittedly, Villa were themselves in the Third Division at that time, but we are talking about THE Aston Villa, winners of the FA Cup a record seven times.

Chico Hamilton was around at the time.

"We were in a depression, there's no doubt about that. We were probably more interested in getting back to the top division but, even so, there was no excuse for our Cup disappointments. We just did not perform when we had to."

Naturally, Villa's Cup progress improved as they also rose up the table and a good FA Cup fourth-round victory over Arsenal in 1974 was a tie to remember. Jim Cumbes was in goal.

"We surprised them at Highbury with a 1-1 draw. They had a very strong side with players like Bob Wilson, Pat Rice, Bob McNab, George Armstrong, Alan Ball, Ray Kennedy and John Radford. We were a goal up at half-time, but they got an equaliser in the second half. There was a crowd of just under 48,000 for the replay which was four days later. It was a great game with a tremendous atmosphere. Sammy Morgan, who had scored for us at Highbury, put us ahead by half-time and, during the break, we talked in the dressing-room and reminded ourselves about what had happened last time. We were not going to make the same mistake again. Arsenal had a real go at us of course, but when Alun Evans made it 2-0 we were confident of being through to the next round and we probably played our best football then even though Arsenal stepped up their performance. Both teams were given a standing ovation at the end. It was that kind of a game — definitely one to remember."

If there were medals for reaching the quarter-finals of the FA Cup, Villa would have had several bins full by now. In the decade of the 1970s they reached that stage twice, Manchester United ending the 1976-77 run and West Ham the 1979-80 campaign. There have been countless visits to the sixth round since then of course.

There was little FA Cup joy in the 1980s, or indeed up to date, but that does not mean there is any lack of ambition.

"I love playing at Wembley and our Coca-Cola Cup success has been great," said Dwight Yorke. "But there is no competition in the world like the FA Cup, and I really want to be playing in the Final some time soon."

Gareth Southgate took a similar view.

"Historians of the game know that Aston Villa has one of the greatest FA Cup pedigrees in the country. The club has been in nine Finals and won seven of them, and is still the third most successful FA Cup clubs of all time. The problem is that there has not been any success for nearly forty years. Our priority is always the Premiership championship, but that takes nothing away from our FA Cup ambitions. In a sense, that is our Holy Grail!"

CHAPTER FOURTEEN

CHAMPIONS!

Over to you, lads!

FINISHING the season as champions might not carry the same sudden-death glamour profile as winning the FA Cup, but it is still the highest honour in the game. Lifting the championship trophy is the sweet reward for months of hard work come rain or shine, injuries, bad refereeing decisions, or anything else that may be planted in the mined road to success.

Aston Villa have been champions of the League no fewer than seven times but, without a doubt, the triumph of the 1980-81 season has to be the greatest championship of them all. Without taking away any of the glory from those who were crowned kings of English football in 1894, 1896, 1897, 1899, 1900 and 1910, those successes were in a totally different world. When Ron Saunders master-minded the championship of 1981, football was massively different and competition was so much the fiercer.

The Villa fans had waited 71 years, endured two World Wars and seen their mighty club among the fallen to Division Three, before at last being able to hold their heads high once again among the elite of English football. Small wonder then that there was such a celebration in May 1981 around Villa Park. Amid a period of Merseyside domination, the Midlands had struck a blow for the rest of the Football League. Villa were undisputed champions.

One man with mixed feelings about the League championship season of 1980-81 is Gordon Cowans, who was delighted that his club had lifted the League title again, but was disappointed with his own contribution.

"Every player dreams of being a member of a championship-chasing team, battling every week at the top of the top division. But that dream nearly turned into a nightmare for me as I went through a really bad playing patch. While my Villa team-mates seemed to play out of their skins every week as we raced against, and beat, Ipswich Town for the title, I was bitterly disappointed with my own form.

"Wherever Villa played they won rave reviews for their fast, attacking style. As for me, after the opening couple of months I could hardly put a foot right. Even now I can't put my finger on the reason for my poor form. I saw Ron Saunders week after week to discuss my problems, but he couldn't explain it either. He just told me to keep battling away. If I gave 100 per cent I would keep my place in the side. I did my best and I did not miss a game all season — but I think, in his shoes, I would have dropped me.

"I'll never forget our home game against Crystal Palace. We won 2-1 but I couldn't do anything right. I continually miscontrolled the ball. I was often caught in possession, and I couldn't even hit a simple square pass to a team-mate a few feet away. The other Villa lads gave me a good-natured ribbing afterwards and it was suggested that I was probably the best

Palace player on the park!"

Of course, Gordon Cowans is underestimating the value of his own great contribution in that season even though he was being genuinely self-critical. He always was prepared to give others the credit and prefers to talk about the great team effort that led to that historic success.

"If I had to list the three main factors that took us to the First Division title I would place the players' fighting spirit as the main quality. Every player was prepared to run and chase for his mates. That tremendous attitude carried us through on many occasions. The second key reason for our success was the all-round ability in the side. From Jimmy Rimmer in goal to Tony Morley out on the left wing, there was a standard set for each player. Every Villa man knew that he could do a good job as an individual and also blend into the team set-up.

"The third vital factor was the Villa men's will to win. You may think that all players go out, week in and week out, determined to end up on the winning side. But when the going gets tough, it's pouring with rain and the pitch is a mud-bath, some teams seem to ease up. Invariably they lose. We kept going!

"There is a great tradition at Aston Villa. The club is one of the oldest and most famous in the world. Too many of the great moments had been in the past and we were determined to make 1981 a year for the history books. I think we succeeded!"

Allan Evans only missed three games as Villa raced to the League title.

"My League championship medal is one of my prized possessions," he said. "It was a great season for us. We worked hard and I think we thoroughly deserved the title. There were some excellent games and possibly we could have had the championship wrapped up earlier than we did. Sometimes though, things don't always fall into place like that. No complaints, we played well all season. Personally I was also delighted for the Villa supporters. They were excellent and never lost faith at any stage."

Dennis Mortimer was captain of that side and he believes that winning the championship is the greatest prize of all.

"It has to be even greater than winning a Cup competition because you have to prove yourself over so many more games. Winning the League Cup and the European Cup were fantastic achievements, but they were still the result of winning a handful of games, rather than being successful over nine months and forty-two games as we were during that season.

"Ron Saunders had been shaping the side for some years. I signed from Coventry in December 1975. Villa had been promoted to the First Division at the end of the previous season and they were having a season of re-establishing themselves in the top division. I had played at Villa Park earlier in the season when they beat us 1-0. Ray Graydon had scored the Villa goal. What I noticed was the great atmosphere there with more than 41,000 people in the ground.

"I was not unhappy at Coventry but Villa seemed to be bursting with ambition and when Ron Saunders made a £175,000 bid, I was more than a little interested in joining his set-up. My debut was at home to West Ham on Boxing Day and there was an even bigger crowd of more than 50,000. We won 4-1 and really played well. I remember thinking, 'this is all right — you're in the right place now Dennis.' I spoke too soon because we lost at Derby on the following day, got knocked out of the FA Cup by Southampton, drew 0-0 at Arsenal and then 1-1 at home to Newcastle — and in that game I was injured and missed the next six matches. It all seemed to be going a bit sour.

"It didn't get much better when I returned to the side. We drew six of the next eight games and lost the other two — which were at Tottenham, where they won 5-2, and at Birmingham of all places, where we lost 3-2. We won our last two games of the season which cheered everyone up and we ended out of danger — but it had been disappointing because Villa had looked capable of a place in the top half of the table rather than the bottom.

"It's interesting to note that, of the team that won the championship, only Gordon Cowans and myself were in the squad that played in Villa's first season back in Division One. Ian Ross and Chris Nicholl were captains before me and they were both excellent leaders and I was flattered to be following them. There were a great many comings and goings in the next few seasons as Ron Saunders sought to perfect his squad. Improvements were beginning to be noticed and certainly our results were much better.

"The following season Chris Nicholl, as captain, lifted the League Cup and we also finished in fourth place in the First Division which pleased everyone. We had some pretty good results that season, finishing with a 4-0 home win over West Bromwich in which Andy Gray hit a hat-trick. It was a great way in which to send everyone off into the summer with a smile and it compensated a little for two League defeats by Birmingham. Still there were only Gordon Cowans and myself in the first team of those who would ultimately win the title.

"Birmingham City beat us again at home and away during the next season and we were beginning to get a bit fed up with them. We progressed to the fourth round of the UEFA Cup and possibly that affected our League form for a while because we finished in eighth place when we really ought to have finished a lot higher. What was really interesting though was that the eventual championship-winning squad was rapidly starting to take shape. Gordon Cowans and I had been joined by Jimmy Rimmer, Allan Evans and Ken McNaught.

"When the 1978-79 campaign started we were just three seasons away from the championship. We knew that things were definitely getting better because we actually beat Birmingham in both our League fixtures. There was a bit of a shock when Andy Gray was sold to Wolves, but we were confident of the fact that our manager knew what he was doing — and since the £1.47 million fee was a British record, we guessed that he would have some serious plans for the money.

"We finished eighth again, but this had been a season of major developments. When we won the title a couple of years later, only fourteen players were used. By the end of that 1978-79 season, nine of those players were in the Aston Villa first team — Gordon Cowans, Allan Evans, Colin Gibson, Ken McNaught, Jimmy Rimmer, Gary Shaw, Kenny Swain, Gary Williams and myself.

"During the following season, Des Bremner, Eamonn Deacy, David Geddis and Tony Morley came into the side and we finished in seventh place. Ron Saunders was never one to waste words but he said that he felt we were on the verge of being the finished article. It was obvious that he also felt that we were still lacking something too. When he signed Peter Withe at the end of that season we all knew that he believed that he had found what he had been looking for.

"At the start of the 1980-81 season I was asked what I thought our chances were. I said that we now had the best Villa side that I had ever played in, that we had enormous skill and that we were serious championship candidates. I know that most people tried not to laugh when I said that, but I also knew that there were a few who actually believed me. When we went to the top of the table those 'Doubting Thomases' began to change their minds. Villa had not been at the top of the First Division since before World War Two.

"We were not easy winners of the championship as there were a number of setbacks, but I will never forget the last day of that season. We were away to Arsenal and the very least we needed was a draw. If we didn't get it then Ipswich could be champions if they got a result at Middlesbrough. About 20,000 Villa supporters turned up at Highbury and, in front of nearly 60,000 people we gave what was probably our worst performance of that season. Absolutely nothing went right and, looking back, I'm sure that it was because we were far too uptight. Our supporters were brilliant as usual and never stopped cheering us on. In the end, though, we lost 2-0 and our heads were really low until the news reached us that Ipswich had failed to get a result at Middlesbrough and we were champions after all. I have never seen such celebrations after a defeat!

"The biggest party came later when we travelled to Birmingham Town Hall to show off the trophy. There were masses of fans everywhere. It was a very proud moment for me as captain and I was also really thrilled for my hard-working team-mates and the Villa supporters who had never stopped believing in us. Many of them had travelled down to Highbury for that last game of the season. On their radios they had heard that Ipswich had taken the lead at Middlesbrough and at the same time they were watching us playing badly as we headed toward defeat. Nevertheless they had not given up! As I held up the trophy and showed it to them I couldn't help but feel that it was really theirs. After waiting 71 years since the previous championship, and after all the support they had given us that season and every season, I felt that they all deserved to have the trophy for themselves.

"As long as I live I shall remember that time and those scenes. I was more than proud to be captain of Aston Villa, champions of England!"

Since that wonderful experience, the championship has eluded the club — although on two occasions it was almost within their grasp.

Graham Taylor had taken over as manager in July 1987 and it almost seemed as if history might be repeating itself. Villa were in the Second Division and needed a restoration job. Within a season they were promoted. The following season they were still rebuilding and had to be content with 17th place in the First Division — one place lower than Villa's last return to the top division.

When the 1989-90 season got under way, Villa did not have the most brilliant start. However, it did get better and by the end of November they were second in the table for the first time in many years. Liverpool were setting the pace but by mid-January Aston Villa were level on points with them and the eyebrows of the so-called 'experts' were being raised even higher. By the middle of March, the "impossible" was beginning to look even more probable as Villa had taken over the leadership with a two point gap between them and Liverpool.

Liverpool, however, moved into a different gear for the title run-in and Villa began to drop a few points. The final outcome was that Liverpool took the championship and Villa finished in the runners-up spot. They were nine points behind but that in no way really reflected the dramas of that season.

"Nobody thought we had the slightest chance of finishing any higher than halfway," said David Platt. "We were confident that we could do much better than that and so everyone worked hard throughout the season. We hit a bit of a bad patch during the second half of the season and, after a long run of home wins, we dropped a few points unexpectedly. While we were having those few games of poor form, Liverpool were improving all the time and I really think that they gained strength from seeing us slip a little. Anyway, at the end of it all, we were able to have pride in the fact that we finished second. We had surprised a lot of people and we were much closer to the championship than many might have realised."

There was an even closer call in the 1992-93 season when Ron Atkinson was in charge. It was the inaugural season for the new Premier League as it was then called. Norwich City had surprised everybody by going eight points clear by the start of December. Villa, Blackburn and Chelsea were the chasing pack. In the middle of February, Villa emerged as leaders as the Premier pack was shuffled.

Villa held on to the leadership, on and off, until the beginning of April. Then Manchester United put together a run of seven victories to the end of the season. Villa faltered and when they lost their last three games there could be only one conclusion. The final gap was ten points, but the race had, in fact, been much closer run than Villa's last placing as runners-up.

"We were a bit sick to be honest," said Ron Atkinson. "We had done all the hard work and for most of the season we were either very close to the top or were actually in the lead. At the end of it all we felt that we had given away the championship rather than having had it wrestled from us. Without trying to take anything at all away from Manchester United, we had been in the driving seat. They had had a terrific end to their season and if only we had kept up our form they still wouldn't have been able to catch us. Football is a cruel game at times. If you are on form you can guarantee that everything will just fall into place. The referee's decisions seem to go with you, the injuries are less, If the ball hits the post it will either go in or rebound to the feet of one of your players but, if your form is down, everything goes against you. Our form slipped, we gave away some really silly goals and that is what cost us the championship that season. We were so near and yet so far!"

So how long will it be before Aston Villa strike Premiership gold and win the title once again?

"I think you have to look at the results since John Gregory took over," said Gareth Southgate. "No disrespect to Brian Little who worked wonders for the club, but when he left a new era began as it always does when a new manager is appointed. What has happened before becomes irrelevant, even though the club did well with the previous manager.

"Under John Gregory we won five of the remaining six games of the season and our confidence went sky-high. There is an exceptional blend of experience at Villa now and there are some excellent young players coming through. I think that the confidence which we have gained from our performances under John Gregory's direction and all his new ideas have lifted the club to a new level. I don't think that anyone can confidently predict what or when they will win because one crucial injury, or even a refereeing decision, can make all the difference in the world. All I can say is that there is a lot of belief at Villa Park that we are very close to major success. Hopefully that will include the championship."

Dwight Yorke might have the answer.

"I don't think that anyone can lift themselves for the big game any better than us. If we can just keep reminding ourselves that every game in the Premiership is a big game, then I believe we can be successful. The championship is a realistic aim for us. As the Premiership becomes stronger and stronger, the title becomes more and more open. Teams like Manchester United will slip up more often and that means that the team that can keep its head and maintain some consistent form throughout the season will be able to take advantage of the decline of their rivals.

"The championship is not just an elusive dream. It is there for the winning and I would not bet against us doing that very soon. Everyone here at Villa Park wants us to begin getting the rewards for our performances. The supporters are willing us to success all the time and you just feel that everything is ready to fall into place. We have the ability and the desire to win the championship and I am absolutely convinced that we are very close to actually doing it!"

EUROPE!

T HERE is not a club in Britain that does not want to be champions of Europe. Very few have actually made it but, of course, Aston Villa are among that elite band of British clubs. Their European campaigns began in 1975 when they were awarded an automatic place in the UEFA Cup as a result of their League Cup success the previous season. However, Villa could have been involved in Europe much earlier. There was a suggestion that the club might like to be involved in a combined team to represent the City of Birmingham in the Inter-Cities Fairs Cup — but Villa declined the offer.

That 1975-76 season was an exciting one for Villa. They were back in the First Division and were holders of the League Cup. Europe was the icing on the cake but unfortunately it was short-lived. Ray Graydon was in both legs of that first-round tie against Antwerp.

"I think we suffered from inexperience. Antwerp were at home in the first leg and took full advantage of it. I scored a consolation goal for us but, apart from that, nothing much went right and Antwerp hit four past us. We played again a fortnight later back at Villa Park but it really was a bridge too far and we never got going. The supporters were great and we felt bad for them. Antwerp scored another and finished as 5-1 winners on aggregate. It was not a great baptism into European football but we learned from it."

Villa's next sortie was two years later. Once again the club had qualified for the UEFA Cup by winning the League Cup. A second bite at the competition was just what they had wanted and their first-round tie against Fenerbahce of Turkey was a far different affair from the previous European attempt two years earlier. Jimmy Rimmer was in goal.

"I had only just joined Villa from Arsenal during the summer. I had had some experience in Europe, mostly from my days with Manchester United when I was deputy to Alex Stepney. I already owned a European Cup medal as a substitute in the 1968 Final, but joining Villa presented a new challenge in Europe.

"We were drawn at home in the first leg against Fenerbahce and the club had learned from Antwerp all about getting a good advantage to take through to the second leg if it was an away game. The fans were up for it and, by the end of the evening, John Deehan had scored twice and Andy Gray and Brian Little had added a goal each to give us a 4-0 lead to take away. John Deehan and Brian Little both scored in the second leg and we won the tie with a 6-0 aggregate. That was a bit of a change from the previous UEFA Cup game and the supporters were really happy. So were we!

"We had Gornik Zabrze in the next round. Once again we were drawn at home first, and this time it was Ken McNaught's turn to grab the headlines when he scored twice to give us a 2-0 lead to take to Poland. So far we had played three games, scored eight and conceded nothing. Andy Gray scored for us in the away leg, but Gornik spoiled our record when they made it 1-1. We were through to the next round though and this time we were drawn against Athletic Bilbao. It was unusual that we were drawn to play the first leg at home once again and so we went into the same routine as before. An own-goal and a goal from John Deehan gave us a 2-0 lead, and in Spain Dennis Mortimer scored as we drew 1-1. I don't think that many people could believe that Aston Villa were in the quarter-finals of the UEFA Cup. We came out of the hat alongside Barcelona and yet again we had to play at home first. They were a tough nut to crack, a little too tough in fact and, even though Ken McNaught and John Deehan gave us what was becoming a customary two goals at home, Barcelona also scored two and the tie was poised at 2-2 when we went to Spain. Brian Little scored for us over there but Barcelona hit two and that was the end of our UEFA Cup campaign. We felt that we had given a reasonable account of ourselves and the supporters were much happier with our efforts.

"We were itching to have another crack at Europe but we were forced to wait another four years before we could try again. It was a very frustrating time because, while you are not involved, you cannot avoid hearing the results and details of those who are and it keeps reminding you that you ought to be competing in Europe yourself."

John Deehan's goals had been a major factor in that UEFA Cup attempt but in the end they counted for nothing.

"It was heart-breaking to go out of the competition at the quarter-final stage. In the first leg at Villa Park, Johann Cruyff had played a blinder until he limped off in the second half. He was at the hub of all Barcelona's moves and helped them to a

2-0 lead. It was only our guts and determination that brought us back into the game. The second leg was set for a real battle and we had our backs to the wall when John Gidman was sent off fairly early on in the game. Even so, Brian Little scored and that put us 3-2 ahead on aggregate. We could not maintain our game, though, and in the second half we cracked and Barcelona scored twice to put the tie out of reach. It was a big disappointment but we had done our best, and the fact that we had come so far in only our second attempt at a European competition gave us heart for the future."

Villa's next European challenge was in the big one — the European Cup. Ron Saunders had masterminded the way into the competition by guiding Villa to the League championship in the 1980-81 season, and now there was the challenge to go where Liverpool and Nottingham Forest between them had dominated for the previous five years.

Once again Jimmy Rimmer was in goal for the whole campaign — well, very nearly the whole campaign!

"We were a bit taken aback when we heard that our first-round tie was against Valur. We had to check the map to confirm that the club was from Iceland. Sure enough, we were drawn to play at home first and, once again, we went out with the intention of winning the game while we had home advantage. We were looked upon as favourites to win the tie and nothing less than a convincing win would do. Ron Saunders prepared us well and, to be fair, the Valur side played very well but we went about our task in a very professional — almost cold — manner and beat them 5-0 on the night. Tony Morley scored the first, Terry Donovan got two, and Peter Withe scored the other two. In the away leg we won 2-0 with Gary Shaw getting both goals.

"We went from the peacefulness of Iceland to the bustle of East Germany for our next round. Our opponents were Dynamo Berlin. Remember that this was when the Berlin Wall was still standing as a kind of prison wall. For a change we were drawn away in the first leg and we did ourselves proud by winning 2-1, thanks to Tony Morley's two goals. We were perhaps a little over-confident on the return leg. Certainly, Dynamo Berlin went about the job with a greater passion and shocked us by winning the game 1-0. Our extra away goal proved to be vital and we were relieved to go into the draw for the next round. We were to play another club from the communist lands, this time it was to be Dynamo Kiev of what was then the USSR. Again we were to play away in the first leg."

However, much was to happen between the second round which was completed at the start of November and the third round which was to be played in March. Ron Saunders, the man who had taken Villa this far on the hunt for European glory, resigned as the club struggled in the First Division. Tony Barton, his assistant, became caretaker-manager first of all and was then confirmed as manager. What a challenge he faced — as he recalled not long before his premature death.

"We had to improve our League results but at the same time we were growing in confidence in Europe and we didn't want to do anything too drastic which could undermine that. I don't think that sweeping changes are necessarily an instant cure. We just tried to keep the morale high and encouraged the players to go about their League programme with the same spirit that they were demonstrating in their European games."

As we have seen, it worked. When Villa resumed the European Cup trail, they did so on the back of four successive Division One games without defeat.

"It had been a huge shock when Ron Saunders left," said Jimmy Rimmer. "But we were all determined to be loyal to the club and its supporters — and of course to Tony Barton. I think we also wanted to see the job through for the sake of Ron who had created the squad that had come this far. We held Dynamo Kiev to a 0-0 draw in the first leg and then went in for the kill at Villa Park a fortnight later. Gary Shaw and Ken McNaught did the business and we won the game and tie 2-0. Now it was getting very exciting as we were through to the semi-finals.

"Anderlecht were the team we had to beat. They had a big reputation and we were reminded that it had been a Belgian club which had ended Villa's first attempt at winning a European competition. We had become much wiser since then however. The first leg was at Villa Park and another huge crowd cheered us on. Tony Morley took the glory that night when he scored the only goal of the game. What a player! Anderlecht just could not keep him under control and that goal really punished them. The tension for the return leg was sensational. Another big crowd roared Anderlecht on, but we were unmovable and I think the defence for that game was probably having one of its best games ever. We held out and the score was 0-0 which meant that we were through to the Final of the European Cup which was to be played in Rotterdam. Our opponents were the mighty Bayern Munich."

Villa were certainly the underdogs for that game. Bayern Munich had already won the European Cup three times and took the role of Goliath in the Final while Villa played David in the hope that one shot slung in might do the job. Again there was an unexpected drama to unfold.

"I had been injured for a while but it was decided that I would start the Final," said Jimmy Rimmer. "We had Nigel

Spink on the bench and we thought that it was most likely that he would have to be used. We didn't tell him that because we didn't want to put pressure on him, after all, he had only played in one League match for Villa and that had been a couple of years earlier. My problem was a neck injury and after ten minutes I indicated to the bench that I could not go on. Nigel replaced me and played brilliantly. I stood to applaud him at the end and then raced on to the pitch to congratulate him and the others. Bayern Munich had thrown everything at him but he had played his heart out and just refused to let anything go past. It was a fantastic performance. We had scored and when the final whistle went it was the German players who slumped to the ground while we, the underdogs, were dancing on clouds.

"When we went up to collect the trophy and our medals it must have seemed a little strange to see two goalkeepers there. For me it was a great thrill to be collecting a second European Cup winners' medal with a different club. Not many people have done that with two different clubs."

It was quite a night for Nigel Spink too.

"I didn't have time to think about what was happening. One minute I was on the bench watching the game and not expecting to become a part of it, and the next minute I was out there between the posts. We were under a lot of pressure from the Germans for much of the game but the defence was in terrific form and gave me a lot of confidence. I gritted my teeth and got on with the job but I was well relieved when the final whistle went. It was a tremendous experience."

For Tony Barton it was an incredible night.

"I mostly remember the final whistle going and realising that we had won. It was a feeling like no other and I am not ashamed to admit that there were tears in my eyes. The players had worked so hard and really deserved their victory — and the supporters had been magnificent all the way through the season. Nobody had expected us to win but we had never written ourselves off. We had the courage to face up to the task and the ability to see it through.

"I think as well, when we brought the trophy back to Birmingham and paraded it around, just how much it meant to that sea of supporters who were so excited about it. It was an amazing time and an experience that has stayed with me as a treasured memory ever since."

It was Peter Withe, of course, who had scored the winner on that fantastic night in Rotterdam.

"I would have been hard pushed to have missed really," he said. "We had been playing for just over an hour when Tony Morley broke down the left flank and sent over a brilliant cross. It landed at my feet just two yards out and all I had to do was sidefoot it home. It was not the best goal that I've ever scored, but it was certainly the most important. I had played in every game leading to the Final and this was the pinnacle of it all. I still get excited when I think about it."

But there was another tale to add to the European Cup night of triumph.

"Two things happened when the game ended. Gary Newbon grabbed me for a quick television interview and that meant that I missed the team photo taken immediately after the game and then, even worse, Ken McNaught and I were summoned by UEFA officials for an obligatory urine test. Two of the Bayern players had to go as well so, while all the lads were enjoying themselves in the dressing-room, we were standing there, desperately trying to oblige the UEFA officials. The trouble is, when you have been running around for an hour and a half on a hot evening, you dehydrate and you can't always provide a sample that easily. We sat there waiting for something to happen. Then I had a brainwave. I saw a bloke walking past with some crates of beer. I asked him where he was going and he said that the beer was for the dressing-rooms. I commandeered a crate and offered the two German players a drink. They refused at first but then decided to call it a day and join in. After about four or five pints each we were at last able to oblige and get back to the dressing-rooms. Everyone had changed by the time we got there and we had a mad rush to get into our suits and board the coach. A few minutes more and they would probably have gone without us. Thank goodness for a few pints of beer!

"Although we won the European Super Cup against Barcelona the following season and lost to Penarol in the World Club championship — both great experiences — there is nothing like playing in the Final of the European Cup. Scoring the winner makes it even more special and that night in Rotterdam will live with me for ever."

Allan Evans missed only one of Villa's European Cup games on the way to that historic triumph of 1982. He was always confident that Villa could take the trophy, even though there was the shock of Ron Saunders' departure.

"Like everyone else at the club, I believed that Ron would be a fixture for a long time to come. That was the only reason that I agreed to a seven-year contract. However, we were a terrific team, so good that our European Cup win wasn't as difficult as some people might imagine. No, I'm not saying that it was easy, but I reckon that trying to win promotion from the Second Division was a lot harder!"

Dennis Mortimer was captain of the side that lifted the

European Cup and still feels the thrill of actually receiving the trophy on that amazing night.

"A lot of hard work went into that success. Bayern Munich were great opponents and we had a lot of respect for them. However there is a difference between respect and fear. We had gone through just as many games as they had to get to the Final and we felt that on the strength of that alone we were at least as good as them. We had a lot of self-respect as well as respect for our opponents.

"We knew they had a lot of talent but we also knew that they would not work any harder than we would and that they could not be any hungrier than us. We really wanted that trophy and we were ready to run ourselves into the ground for it."

Villa's work-rate was phenomenal and nobody grafted more than Mortimer who, as captain, kept the team on their toes throughout while putting in his own masterly performance that was the epitome of leading by example. When the final whistle blew, excitement took over from energy.

"We were so tired that I remember hoping that the trophy would not be too heavy," laughed Mortimer. "Yet there was enough left in the tank for us to be able to commiserate with the Bayern lads, collect our medals, and go on a lap of honour. It is difficult to describe what you feel the actual moment that you lift the trophy. You just do it! It is placed in your hands and you can't wait to lift it as high as possible to show the fans their prize. It is a very emotional moment. Your brain doesn't really take it in until later and it is only then that you realise that you have made an indelible mark in football history. Nobody can ever take your achievement away and you feel both very proud and very emotional. I remember thinking, 'We've done it, we've actually done it! We've won the European Cup. Bloody hell! We've won the European Cup!'

"What really brought it home was seeing Ron Saunders with a smile on his face. I knew then that it was not just a dream!"

Villa have been back in Europe since then but, up to now, they have not managed to repeat that tremendous achievement of 1982 — although there are a few encouraging signs. English clubs are becoming more and more street-wise in European competition and Villa are among the front-runners of those who have recently impressed.

That European Super Cup victory over Barcelona, mentioned above, deserves more than just the passing mention it has been afforded. It was played in January 1983. Barcelona had been winners of the European Cup-winners' Cup and were confident that they could repeat their victory over Villa of several years earlier. They were wrong! They won the first leg 1-0, but it was not a convincing victory and when the two teams met again at Villa Park a week later, Villa showed them who was the boss. Gary Shaw, Gordon Cowans and Ken McNaught all scored a goal each to win 3-0 and record an aggregate 3-1 success which confirmed Villa as undisputed Kings of Europe. It made up for the disappointment of the World Club championship a month earlier, when Villa lost 2-0 to Penarol in Tokyo.

"We were disappointed to have gone all the way to Japan just to lose a game that we felt we should have won," said Dennis Mortimer. "It made us all the more determined not to slip up against Barcelona and we were much more business-like in that tie. We were good value against Barcelona in Spain in the first leg, but we lost. For that reason we were not going to settle for anything less than a good victory in the return — and that is exactly how it worked out."

The defence of the European Cup the following 1982-83 season began well enough, but it fizzled out just when it was getting exciting again. Gary Shaw was the goal hero of that European campaign.

"I was having a good season all round really. With service from Tony Morley and Gordon Cowans, and playing alongside Peter Withe, I was presented with a good many scoring chances. I ended the season as our top scorer in the League and managed to grab a few goals in the European games as well. It started when we played Besiktas of Turkey in the first round. We played at home in the first leg but because there had been some crowd problems it was decided that we would have to play the first leg behind closed doors, which made it a bit weird. We won 3-1 though, with Peter Withe, Tony Morley and Dennis Mortimer getting our goals. We drew 0-0 away so we went into the next round against Dinamo Bucharest. The first leg was in Romania in front of about 70,000 fans and we played very well in difficult circumstances to win 2-0. I scored both goals so I was pretty pleased with that. I was delighted with the return leg as well because we won 4-2, making it a 6-2 aggregate. Dinamo put up quite a fight. I got a hat-trick which has since become one of my most treasured memories. Mark Walters scored our other goal and the important thing was that we were through to another round and still had our hands on the trophy.

"It all went wrong in the next round, which was the quarter-final. Of all people, we were drawn against Juventus, who ultimately went on to play in the Final. Our first leg was at home and they beat us 2-1. Gordon Cowans scored an excellent goal for us but Juventus were on top form. We thought we were still in with a chance in the second leg but, with 66,000 Italians cheering them on, Juventus took their chances and won 3-1. Peter Withe scored our goal which made the aggregate score 5-2 to Juventus. It was a long haul back from Italy knowing that we were no longer holders of the European Cup. I'm sure Villa will be there again before long."

Villa have taken heart from their most recent UEFA campaign. Their performances in Europe have proved that they are more than capable of living in such talented company. Gareth Southgate played a major part in the campaign.

"I think we surprised ourselves by going as far as we did in the 1997-98 UEFA Cup competition. We seemed to play better in the UEFA Cup than we did in the Premiership until the latter part of the season. We played four very good European teams and it would have been no disgrace to go out to any one of them. We reached the quarter-finals and, to be honest, we were disappointed not to get through. The achievement of getting that far was forgotten on the night.

"We have given it some thought since and have come to realise that the experience of playing against some of the best players in the world was of great benefit to us. We learned a great deal and we feel that we are more than capable of getting even further in the competition. I don't really think it will be that long before the name of Aston Villa will be on one of the European trophies."

Stan Collymore is even more determined.

"The way that we play is suited for European competition. I enjoy the occasions and the travelling. It is a great experience every time that you play, whether at home or away. Sometimes the supporters of the club that you are visiting can get a bit volatile — depending upon which part of Europe that you happen to be visiting — but we stick together and we are usually well looked after by the officials.

"I love playing in European competitions and I am sure that there is only one thing anyone could enjoy better — winning one!"

REFLECTIONS

THERE have been many great Villa players and personalities in the last half century, far too many for us to be able to include all of them in this book. There have been many great games too and no doubt many readers will have their own particular favourites. Have you ever wondered, though, how others perceive Aston Villa?

"I always think of a big club that is always likely to win the championship," said John Barnes. "Villa Park is a lovely ground and if you come away with a result you know you have done well because it is the sort of place where the supporters lift the home team so much that you have an uphill task before you have even started. Aston Villa is a club with a great history, a club that has earned respect. It will never be too far from the leaders. Like every other club, Villa has had its ups and downs — but write off Aston Villa at your peril!"

Denis Law had many a fine battle with Villa, both with Manchester United and City, his two major clubs in English football. He also had a sneaking admiration for Villa.

"You can't help but admire them. Villa Park has always been

a great ground and it is a rare Villa side that doesn't play good football. I don't think that I have ever met someone who actually dislikes Aston Villa. Nobody likes to be beaten by them of course, but they are a fine club with absolutely super support."

Allan Clarke played for Leeds against Villa many times and has vivid recollections of the games involving the two clubs.

"We had some terrific tussles and the two clubs still have a tradition of exciting matches. I remember playing against Villa when I was with Fulham and Leicester as well and, no matter which club you are with, you will find that the team-talk is always a little bit more tense when Aston Villa are involved. They have to be among the top six clubs in the country and they command that sort of respect!"

David Batty has also seen action against Villa with each of his three clubs to date — Leeds, Blackburn and Newcastle United.

"I really enjoy going to Villa Park because it is such a lovely ground. The club has a great atmosphere and there is always a friendly welcome. It is one of those clubs where you feel at home very quickly and where, in a 30,000 crowd, you feel that everyone knows everyone else."

The above are just a few opinions from various people, but you could ask anyone in the game and you would find it extremely difficult to discover anyone with a bad word to say about Aston Villa. Why is there so much respect for the club? The word 'tradition' is probably the link, but there has to be a beginning to any tradition and also a point to it. In Aston Villa's case the tradition comes with age, size, support and success.

"The club has an amazing history," says Johnny Dixon. "Aston Villa did the double before most people even knew there was such a thing."

That fact is not lost on Dennis Mortimer.

"It came home to me that although the club was more than a hundred years old when I was made skipper, there had probably been well under a hundred captains during that time. I felt honoured to be entrusted with such a position. It was like being made head of the family for my generation. When you are at Villa Park you know that the walls are dripping with the memories of great games, great players, the cheers of fans who were following in the footsteps of their fathers, their grand-fathers and their great-grandfathers, tears of victory and defeat, and the roars of success. It is fantastic! I think that is one of the reasons why Aston Villa is so special. It has a living history. When you visit a stately home somewhere you get that same feeling of tradition and history. The difference with Aston Villa and Villa Park is that it is also still very much alive and kicking!"

Reg Thacker is Villa's archivist and historian. He loves being surrounded by both the past and the present. In his spare time he is also a member of the 'George Formby Society' and likes nothing better than to bring back to life the songs and music of that great entertainer. He looks upon his vast collection of Villa memorabilia in the same way.

"Villa has had some wonderful entertainers down the years. Some were jugglers, some made you laugh, others even made you cry sometimes, but they were all a part of this great show that we call Aston Villa, and they all played the sort of football that was magical and made a kind of music. They come back to life through our collection of photographs, programmes, film footage and newspaper cuttings. They also come back to life in a more real way through today's players and the supporters. As long as the club lives there will be a continuation of this great tradition that is Aston Villa. The names and the faces may change, but the family goes on and on!"

There have been several occasions when the "family" came close to death. The nutrition of football clubs is not its players or its fans — it is money! A shortage of cash has meant death by starvation for many clubs over the years. A few times Villa has appeared to be terminally ill but has been saved by an emergency operation. Doug Ellis has proved to be a brilliant surgeon.

Ellis is one of those people who simply cannot be ignored. "Deadly Doug" they call him, though not many do that to his face. Why is he called that? Well, he has obviously trodden on a few toes in his time, but you must speak as you find. Tommy Docherty, the perennial court jester, once said, "The Villa chairman, Doug Ellis, said he was right behind me. I told him I'd sooner have him in front of me where I could see him." That's one side of the story. Personally I prefer my own.

I was once waiting at the Villa Park reception for an appointment. Mr Ellis came in and said, "Good morning, are you being taken care of?" A few words that spoke volumes. He did not know me at all. I could have been the chief executive of a potential sponsor or just a passing Birmingham City fan needing to visit the loo. It didn't make any difference. I was warmly greeted and the club was professionally represented.

In November 1968 things were pretty desperate at Villa Park. The team was getting closer to the Third Division and there were debts of £500,000. Enter a new board of directors headed by a Birmingham travel agent who was at that time a director of rivals, Birmingham City. This was by no means the first time that there had been problems like this at Villa. In 1955 for instance, shareholders and supporters were united in demanding action as the club faced relegation. In 1968, however, it was quite different. The financial structure of the club was being shaken, extinction was a very definite possibility.

The Birmingham travel agent was, of course, Doug Ellis — and the changes at the club were immediate. The new board moved in on 14 December, cash was injected and Tommy Docherty was appointed manager.

"I am not unaware of the formidable task I have before me," said Doug Ellis. "We will not be relegated. My first job is to establish a resurgence of enthusiasm. I would like to think that our fans will be able to persuade their wives that Aston Villa Football Club are going to be more important than Christmas shopping next Saturday when we intend to beat Norwich City."

It was a bold statement, especially since Ellis had only just divested himself of his link with Birmingham City. It did work though. The team was inspired to beat Norwich and the fans were motivated to turn up in their thousands and give Villa a sharp increase at the turnstiles. Encouraged, fund-raising schemes were launched by the club and a commercial manager was appointed for the first time. Eric Woodward was that man and he played a major role in the Villa revival. The chief energiser, however, was Doug Ellis.

On the field things did get worse before they started getting better. In the boardroom they got better before they got worse. As the 1972-73 season was commencing, the growing tensions and battles in the boardroom reached a showdown and Ellis was voted out of his role as chairman. He remained a director of course and eventually fought his way back as chairman.

The boardroom battles did not end there. Doug Ellis believed that the shareholders and supporters needed a figurehead — a Bertram Mills or a Billy Smart, with whom there could be some identification. With that recognition came responsibility, something on which Ellis thrived. Other board members did not agree and once again Ellis was replaced — this time by Sir William Dugdale. It was 1975 when Sir William took the chair and it was in 1978 that he was replaced by Harry Kartz. Ellis was still there, still campaigning. In December 1982 he became chairman again.

The progress that Villa has made since then is largely due to the amazing effort that he has made, the personal interest he has shown in everything and everybody, and his indefatigable leadership. Now well into his seventies he shows no sign of slowing down.

"My family and I have dedicated ourselves to Aston Villa. We love the club and we have worked hard to bring it success. We intend to continue doing so for as long as we are able."

Few people have worked harder for the club, or indeed for the game, a fact that had not escaped the notice of football fan John Major, who sent this message when he was Prime Minister, on the occasion of the chairman's seventieth birthday: "It can be said of few people that they have left an indelible impression on their chosen walk of life. There is no question but that Doug Ellis is one of those few."

It was appropriate that the man who finally made it as "Mr Aston Villa" had the Wilton Lane stand named after him. Had it not been for his stand against adversity the 'Doug Ellis Stand' might never have happened. Indeed, the famous football pitch might now be buried under a Villa Park housing estate!

Instead of that, the club has survived and thrived and has the financial clout to compete at the highest level in the transfer market.

"Whatever happens we shall always continue to be in the market for big-name players. Obviously other clubs want to keep their best players so we can't just go out and buy who we want when we want. It is no good buying run-of-the-mill players either because we don't want to sign players who are not any better than the stars we already have. Despite that, we never refuse a penny when it is needed!"

That, of course, brings us right back to the question of money. Every week top players are taking home tens of thousands of pounds. Stars of yesterday simply cannot comprehend that kind of money.

"I wonder what they do with it all," said Johnny Dixon. "I just cannot come to terms with it. The sort of money that we earned is roughly what they give to taxi drivers as tips. Good luck to them — I'm not complaining. We were happy enough in our day. When we picked up an extra quid for a win we felt quite well off. Life was very different then."

Trevor Ford also recalled the old days of low pay and transfer abuse.

"Aston Villa showed a decent attitude when I joined them from Swansea. I was being sold for £13,500 which was a decent sum in 1947. Swansea offered me a share — £10! I was expected to move house from Swansea to Birmingham on £10. I appealed to Villa and they stepped in with real help. The only thing I didn't like was the unofficial payments. I was to get an under-the-counter fiver for every goal I scored. I received it by playing snooker against the manager. We would bet and I always won, and that way I was handed my bonus — Crazy!

"In those days my wage was £15 a week during the season and £12 a week in the summer. When I moved to Sunderland I was given a job in a garage. That way I could be paid £25 a week.

I had to work in the garage but had football time off whenever necessary."

It was not just a different time, it was a different world.

It was also a different world in the last century when Villa were involved in a couple of incidents that could not possibly happen today. In 1892, Villa were leading 1-0 against Stoke when they conceded a penalty. Dunning, the Villa goalkeeper, knew there was little time left before the ninety minutes were over, so he kicked the ball out of the ground. By the time the ball had been retrieved the time was up. It was this incident which gave birth to referees being able to add time on for stoppages.

In 1888, Villa were playing Darwen in the FA Cup quarter-final. Villa were 3-0 ahead when the whistle went for half-time. The Villa players had an attack of over-confidence in the dressing-room and opened a bottle of champagne. They spent the second half holding on as Darwen pulled back to 3-2. Needless to say, that champagne had gone straight to the heads of the Villa players. They held on, but they could have been arrested for being in charge of a football while under the influence!

Today's football is not without its curiosities and humour, much of which comes from the things people say. Stan Colly-more went on record as saying, "I'm no angel, but I think I'm misunderstood more than anything else. I'm a pretty interesting bloke!" He has since been proved right.

Tony Daley's haircuts were often a source of hysterical laughter among the Holte Enders. With a perfectly straight face, Daley said, "I get a lot of stick for my haircuts, but you'll always find that within a couple of weeks there's a few kids around who have copied them." Mark Draper has exactly the same problem!

Ron Atkinson is always good for a few choice words to brighten up his image. On the eve of the 1994 League Cup Final he modestly declared, "Just think, Barbra Streisand and Ron Atkinson at Wembley in the same year. What a great season they are having!"

West Ham manager, Harry Redknapp, was amazed by Atkinson.

"The only relaxed boss is Big Ron. He had me drinking pink champagne — before the match!" he said.

Big Ron never really saw himself in the Champagne Charlie mould, but he had a dig at some of his players when he said, "There are one or two players about who would like the competition renamed as the Vodka and Coca-Cola Cup!"

Doug Ellis once said of Ron Atkinson, "I believe Ron to be one of the top three managers in the country." Three weeks later Ron was fired!

It was a time for odd quotes as the word from Brian Little on his resignation from Leicester shows: "I wish to make it clear that I will not be the next manager of Aston Villa." Four days later he was appointed!

Those are typical of the things said and done every week in professional football and especially at Villa Park where the atmosphere remains light-hearted even when there is a period of pressure at the club. Family unity prevails throughout.

For the players, once they have pulled on a Villa shirt, they are considered to be family members for life. Neil Rioch has more than 300 names on his list of members of the Aston Villa Former Players' Association.

"Everyone likes to stay in touch. There is a constant demand for former players to attend functions, and we also have our own football team which has a continual list of charity fixtures. It is quite amazing to see some of them in action. It makes you wonder why they ever stopped playing!"

The Former Players' Association and the demand on those players for autographs and personal appearances demonstrates quite clearly the charisma of Aston Villa Football Club. We have met many of those players through these pages and shared in some of their experiences. The danger is that, if you are not much of a fan before you get to know the club and its great family, you will soon be bitten by the bug.

It is probably best summed up by the words of one anonymous supporter who was once asked why he could not resist cheering on his team. He shrugged his shoulders, gripped the claret and blue scarf around his neck, and said, "I don't know. Once a Villa man, always a Villa man!"

INDEX

BV - #0047 - 280426 - C0 - 234/156/12 - PB - 9781780914718 - Gloss Lamination